JOSÉ CLEMENTE OROZCO
AN AUTOBIOGRAPHY

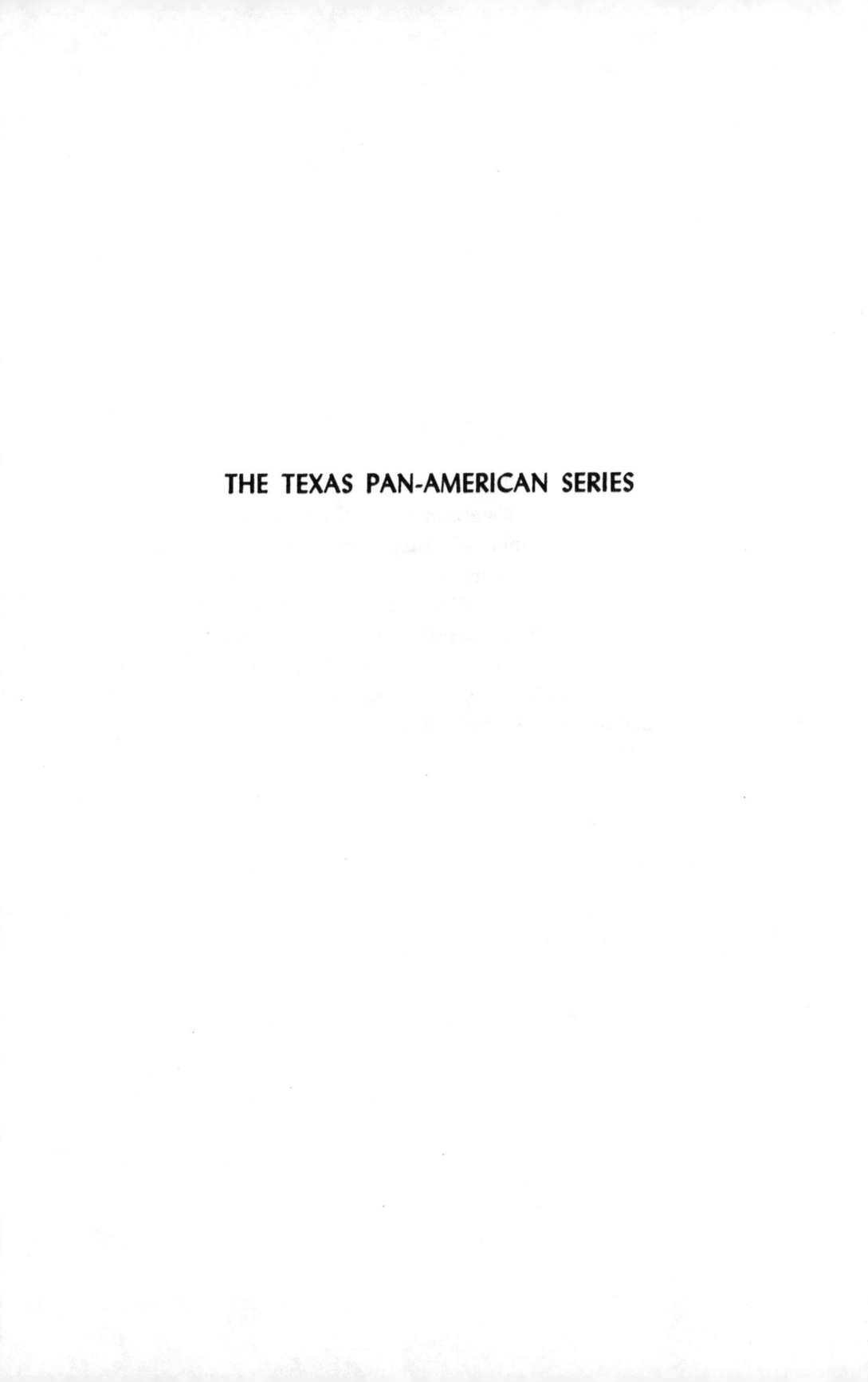

THE TEXAS PAN-AMERICAN SERIES

THE TEXAS PAN-AMERICAN SERIES
is published with the assistance of
a revolving publication fund established by the
Pan-American Sulphur Company and other
friends of Latin America in Texas. Publication of
this book was also assisted by a grant from the
Rockefeller Foundation through the Latin American translation program of the Association of
American University Presses.

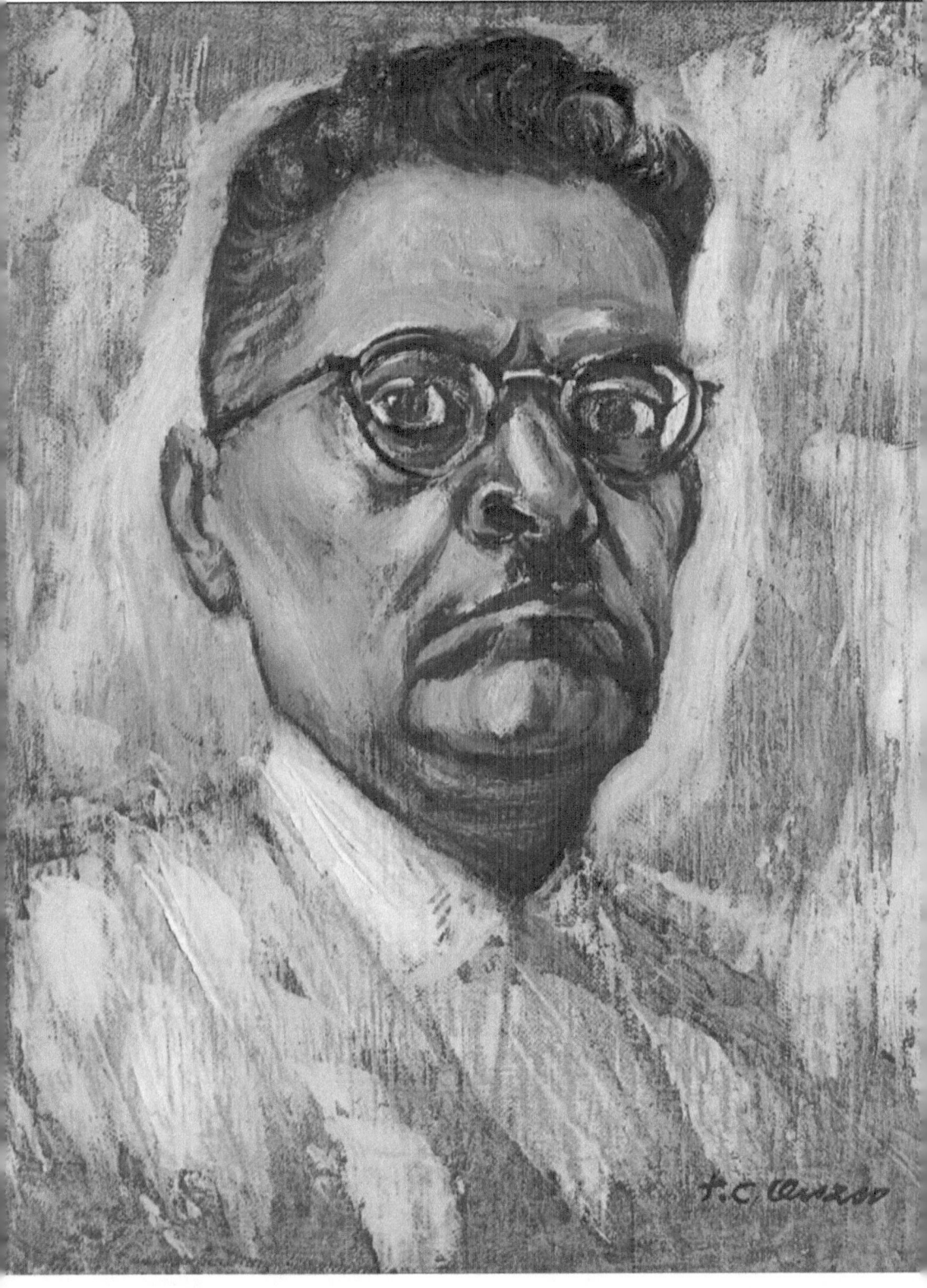

JOSÉ CLEMENTE

Orozco

AN AUTOBIOGRAPHY

Translated by ROBERT C. STEPHENSON

Introduction by JOHN PALMER LEEPER

UNIVERSITY OF TEXAS PRESS • AUSTIN

Requests for permission to reproduce material from this work
should be sent to:
  Permissions
  University of Texas Press
  P.O. Box 7819
  Austin, TX 78713-7819
  http://utpress.utexas.edu/index.php/rp-form

Library of Congress Catalog Number 62-9790

ISBN 978-0-292-76633-4, paperback
ISBN 978-0-292-76634-1, library e-book
ISBN 978-0-292-76635-8, individual e-book

First paperback printing, 2014

ACKNOWLEDGMENTS

The publishers are grateful to Sra. Margarita V. de Orozco for permission to introduce her late great husband's autobiography to the English-speaking world. Gratitude is likewise due to Sr. Clemente Orozco, son of the artist, for invaluable assistance in obtaining the photographs of drawings and paintings with which this book is illustrated. Many of these paintings and drawings are from the Orozco family collection; a number of them have never before been reproduced. Clemente Orozco also reviewed the completed translation, with the assistance of his friend Miss Nina Zoss B., of Malibu, California, and offered a number of helpful suggestions.

CONTENTS

LIST OF ILLUSTRATIONS

xii

Detail from fresco in the Jalisco Hall of Deputies, Guadalajara. 1948–1949. Photo by J. V. Arauz.

Direct working drawing for head of Christ. 23½" x 18¾". Pencil. Orozco Exhibition, Museum of Modern Art, November 1961–January 1962. Photo Soichi Sunami. Courtesy Museum of Modern Art.

INTRODUCTION

Between 17 February and 8 April, 1942, the Mexico City periodical *Excelsior* published in fifteen installments the autobiographical articles which the great Mexican artist, José Clemente Orozco, previously had dictated to his wife, Margarita. These were his first, and were to remain his most important, pronouncements on art and on his life and times, and, as such, each installment was awaited eagerly by an admiring nation. Subsequently, in 1945, the articles were published in book form by *Ediciones Occidente* under the title of *Autobiografía*. The present publication is the first appearance in English of this vivid document, important alike to the bibliography of modern art and to that of contemporary history.

Orozco was a proud, reticent man whose business was painting and whose life was devoid of theatrics. As he submitted his memoirs he wrote, "there is nothing of special interest in it, no famous exploits or heroic deeds, no extraordinary or miraculous happenings. Only the uninterrupted and tremendous efforts of a Mexican painter to learn his trade and find opportunities to practice it." The drama remains implicit. He does not discuss his professional frustrations or his financial problems; he does not indulge in personal rancor; and his beloved family is not even mentioned.

This is not to suggest that Orozco is noncommunicative. Indeed he is exceedingly illuminating and eloquent, but the tone of the *Autobiography* is formal and impersonal. The complete story of Orozco is not to be read in these valuable pages alone; ultimately one will need to refer to his still unpublished letters, to reports of personal conversations, to family records, and to the often highly colored memoirs of his friends and his enemies.

But despite his lean, even taciturn style, and despite the areas he does not touch, Orozco's *Autobiography* is perhaps the most authentic and telling account of the rise of a new national school of painting, and a tale doubly significant in being related by the greatest painter the Americas have produced. Moreover, it is a moving human document, touching in its modesty and understatement.

Except for its concluding paragraphs the *Autobiography* deals principally with his exhaustive training, his association with the Syndicate of Painters and Sculptors, and the frescoes in the National Preparatory School. Orozco first visited the United States in 1917, and again from 1927 to 1934. A considerable portion of the *Autobiography* is devoted to the latter interlude, which saw the creation of the Pomona frescoes, those of the New School for Social Research, and those of Dartmouth College. In 1934 he returned to Mexico to execute in Guadalajara the three fresco cycles which remain without parallel in the western world, and which he refers to only by remarking that he spent four years in Guadalajara "engrossed in intense and fruitful labor." The *Autobiography* thus does not touch upon his most creative years, when his painting was most highly developed and was given an appropriate stage.

We are perhaps particularly interested in his observations about art, and in his political philosophy as defined by the revolutionary epoch he experienced.

Orozco was a rigorously trained artist, a fact unrealized even by his astute biographers until the first appearance of the *Autobiography*. Slowly he developed his powerful individual style, firmly based on academic discipline, without reference to prevailing European theories. Orozco was no fauvist, no cubist, no futurist, in many ways not even a modern artist—except in the German, as opposed to the French, tradition. In this, as in so many instances, he provides a sharp contrast with Diego Rivera.

He describes his severe training at the Academy of San Carlos minutely, with respect rather than with the art student's traditional intolerance and impatience. He had, indeed, little patience with untrained, naive art, dismissing the interest in primitives as "Infantilism," and terming the widely admired Pulque-Shop painting "humbug." As a professional artist he had no interest in the amateur's expression of himself.

Orozco rejected Alfredo Ramos Martínez' re-creation of

Barbizon in Mexico, himself preferring "black and the colors exiled from impressionist palettes." In this he was spurred by the profound influence of the corrosive engravings of Guadalupe Posada, one of the few mentors he acknowledged. It is not the decorative skill or the folk quality of Posada's Calaveras that foreshadow the terrifying passages of the Government Palace frescoes in Guadalajara: it is his trenchant clarity, simplicity, and intensity. And like Posada, Orozco also worked as a political cartoonist.

The 1910 watercolors of brothels, which are among the earliest of his work still existing, are not dissimilar in tonality and style to the Picassos of 1903–1906 (which he could not possibly have seen), but they are less contrived, more biting, and they are untouched by sentimentality. Orozco seems to have had very little curiosity about contemporary art, making no critical comments on either Siqueiros or Rivera, and nowhere does he mention painting in the United States, which concurrently was following an intellectual development not dissimilar to his own. Yet despite his utter independence of European influences, and in particular that of his fellow Titan, Orozco is to speak admiringly of a 1932 Picasso retrospective exhibition in Paris which he saw, and from which he took pains to send a catalogue to his sponsor Alma Reed.

Orozco, like Picasso, uses the human form as the primary expressive agent. He is not so inventive as Picasso in so doing, but fully as eloquent. Orozco was not so sharply concerned with the stylistic manner of his painting as with its constantly mounting power and conviction. But he held special views on the artist's convictions in the realm of politics and wrote: "No artist has, or ever has had, political convictions of any sort. Those who profess to have them are not artists."

A humanitarian he certainly was, deeply sensitive to man's inhumanity to his fellow man, but he was not a politician nor an active party member for any faction. In painting he had scant talent for individualization; in politics he was unable to express his convictions through the dogma of a party. His painting is devoid of individuals. He creates types, identifies their meaningful gestures, but they remain anonymous and faceless. In this he is most similar to the Goya of *Los Caprichos* and *Los Proverbios,* in which the singular instant, or the specific point of view, is obliterated, and what remains is his anguish that war and murder and injustice occur. Much the same thing can be said of Daumier, for today we have forgotten the exact incidents that inspired his incomparable lithographs—only the always applicable, telling comment on humanity is there. But Orozco is never amusing; his irony is deep and bitter.

World War I, the stock market crash, are no more unique and important than the flea circus, which he describes minutely. Good and evil do exist, and while the one is to be celebrated and the other deplored, they are not personified. Orozco was a formal, reticent individual. However passionately he felt he makes no personal revelations, either in paint or in print. He does not participate in recrimination or in resentment on a personal basis; his feelings were much more abstract, and he took positions based on principle rather than become involved personally in the issue. Orozco, like Balzac, saw a vast human comedy, gay and diverting, but one on which he takes no editorial position.

This, of course, has nothing to do with Orozco's eloquence and majesty as an artist. The great frescoes in Guadalajara have a scale, a power, and an intensity that in comparison make a large portion of contemporary art seem decorative and mannered. There is much justification for considering Orozco the major artist of the twentieth century. Certainly he is one of that small handful of Titans who have made our century the most creative in modern history.

JOHN PALMER LEEPER
Marion Koogler McNay Art Institute

JOSÉ CLEMENTE OROZCO
AN AUTOBIOGRAPHY

PRESENTATION

I submit this summary account of much of my life to the review *Occidente*. There is nothing of special interest in it, no famous exploits or heroic deeds, no extraordinary or miraculous happenings. Only the uninterrupted and tremendous efforts of a Mexican painter to learn his trade and find opportunities to practice it. For the most part I have lived in the so-called revolutionary epoch, in that ferociously warring time of frightful convulsions which could very well have ended in the mountain's giving birth to the mouse and was, in any case, most diverting.

May the *Occidente* be the image of our most ardent desires and lofty thoughts.

José Clemente OROZCO

Chapter 1 Posada Inspires Me. San Carlos. Fabrés.

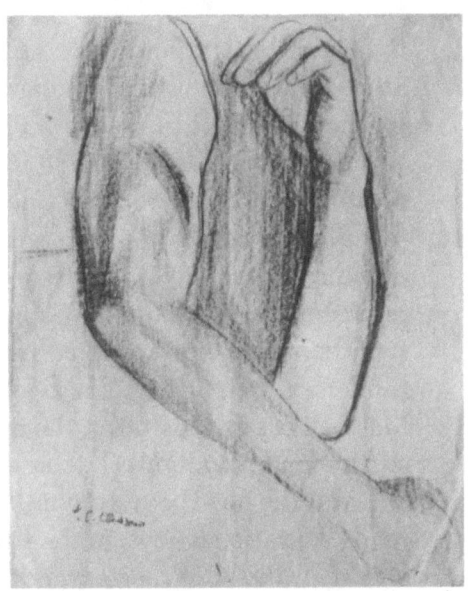

Right Arm and Left Forearm, Study for
Ancient Races. Ca. 1926.

I was born on November 23, 1883, in Ciudad Guzmán or, as it is otherwise known, in Zapotlán el Grande, in the state of Jalisco.

When I was two years old my family moved from Ciudad Grande to Guadalajara, and after a brief stay there to Mexico City. This was sometime in 1890. In the same year I entered the primary school attached to the Teachers College. The College was housed in a building on Licenciado Verdad Street which since that

7

time has been the home successively of the School of Higher Studies, the Publishing Department of the Secretariat of Education, and the Faculty of Philosophy and Letters.

A short way down the street Vanegas Arroyo had his printing press, where José Guadalupe Posada did the famous engravings.

Vanegas Arroyo, as nearly everyone remembers, was the publisher of extraordinary popular works, all the way from story books for children to *corridos,* or current ballads, forerunners, these, of the "extra" editions of newspapers, and Master Posada illustrated them all with engravings which still find many imitators but have never been surpassed.

It was the newsboys' responsible job to hawk Vanegas Arroyo's sensational news in the streets and plazas of the city, and they did it in correspondingly noisy and scandalous terms: "Execution of Captain Cota," or "Horrible Crime of the Most Horrible Son who killed his Horrible Mother."

Posada used to work in full view, behind the shop windows, and on my way to school and back, four times a day, I would stop and spend a few enchanted minutes in watching him, and sometimes I even ventured to enter the shop and snatch up a bit of the metal shavings that fell from the minium-coated metal plate as the master's graver passed over it.

This was the push that first set my imagination in motion and impelled me to cover paper with my earliest little figures; this was my awakening to the existence of the art of painting. I became one of the most faithful customers in Vanegas Arroyo's retail shop, there near the corner of Guatemala and República de Argentina, in a building later torn down in the course of archeological diggings.

In the retail shop Posada's engravings were decorated by hand, and it was in watching this operation that I received my first lessons in the use of color.

I was not long in learning that only a couple of blocks away from the Normal School, in the Academy of Fine Arts of San Carlos, there were night courses in drawing, and I enrolled with great enthusiasm. At the time the patio of the Academy was open, but the corridors were enclosed in glass, and the walls were hung with a countless number of Julien's famous lithographs, the quintessence of academicism, which were to be copied with the utmost care and neatness by whoever wished to study there. A harsh and needless discipline.

In 1897 my family sent me to the School of Agriculture in San Jacinto for the three years' course of an agricultural expert. I was never interested in agriculture and never became an expert, but the education I received in that magnificent school was of great practical value, for the first money I ever earned was for drawing topographical maps, and I might perhaps have been able to plan an irrigation system or build a stable or yoke oxen and plow deep furrows in a straight line. I did know, pretty well, how to sow maize, alfalfa, and cane, and I could analyze soil and treat it. In a word, I was equipped to exploit the land. I had spent three healthy, happy years in the country.

Aspiring to something higher on leaving the School of Ag-

9

riculture, I chose to enter the National Preparatory School, where I remained for four years with the vague intention of studying architecture later, but my obsession with painting led me to drop my preparatory studies and return to the Academy after a few years, this time with a sure knowledge of my vocation.

Since my father had died, I earned my own way through the Academy. I occasionally did drawings for architects. For a while I was a draftsman in the printing shop for *El Imparcial* and others of Reyes Spíndola's publications. It is from this time that I have grateful memories of Carlos Alcalde, an able illustrator and an excellent person.

The Academy was then at its peak in efficiency and organization. It moved with new life under the direction of Antonio Fabrés, a great academic painter from Spain, brought in, as I remember, by Justo Sierra, Minister of Public Instruction, to take complete charge of the Department of Painting.

On his arrival he exhibited numerous works of his in the halls of the Academy, where they caused a sensation among the artists and intellectuals of the city, for they revealed a profound grasp of technique and an unusual ability. They were mostly religious works and genre studies, greatly influenced by Velázquez and similar Spanish painters. At once many disciples gathered round him, and he himself began to work in a large studio assigned to him in the Academy.

Fabrés refashioned the halls for night classes, installing special furniture and equipment to facilitate the work. The

10

electric lighting was perfect, and it was possible to pose a live model or place a plaster one in any desired position or lighting, thanks to ingenious machinery like that of a modern theatre.

To dress the models he had brought a great store of costumes from Europe—armor, plumes, uniforms, cloaks, and other items of carnival garb which were then very much in fashion in the work of academic painters. With these disguises one could paint to the life the musketeers, bull fighters, pages, odalisques, pert street girls, nymphs, bandits, bullies, and the rest of the countless picturesque types so dear to the artists and the public of the last century.

Among Master Fabrés' favorite pupils I should mention Saturnino Herrán, an unmistakably promising student who would have come to be a notable artist in the Mexico of today.

Others who studied in his classes, or at least attended, were Diego Rivera, Benjamín Caria, the Garduño brothers, Ramón López, Francisco de la Torre, Francisco Romano Guillemín, and Miguel Angel Fernández.

Fabrés' method was less a way of teaching than an intense training and a rigorous discipline after the norms of European academies. Nature was to be copied with the greatest photographic exactness, at no matter what expense of time or effort. One and the same model, in one and the same position, faced the students for weeks and even for months, without the slightest variation. Even the shadows were traced in chalk to make sure of keeping the lighting the same throughout. And when the students had copied a particular model for a number of weeks, a photograph was made of it and they compared their efforts with this.

Another frequent exercise was to copy a plaster model in full face, the Venus of Milo, for example.

By these means, and working day and night for years on end, the future artists learned how to draw. They really learned how to draw; there was no doubt about it.

I myself entered the Academy only six months before Master Fabrés returned to Europe. I frequented his studio without, properly speaking, being one of his students, but long enough to realize what it meant to study painting, and I worked tenaciously, furiously, determined to reach my goal cost what it might. So it went for several years.

There was no charge for the model. There were materials, a superb collection of old masters, a great library of books on art. In painting, anatomy, perspective, and the history of art the teachers were good. Above all, there was unrivalled enthusiasm. What more could one want?

Chapter 2 Dr. Atl and Julio Ruelas. Artistic Colonialism. The Revolution in Mexican Painting. Copying Velázquez.

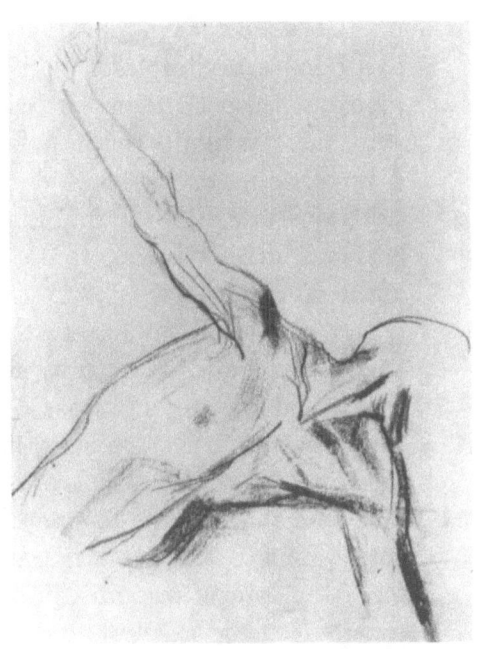

Man Striking. 1930.

s I remember it I first heard of Dr. Atl in connection with a lively public debate that he was carrying on with Julio Ruelas' friends. This must have been one of the many collisions between the Romantics and the Modernists. Ruelas was a painter of cadavers, satyrs, drowned men, and spectral lovers returning from a suicide's grave, whereas Dr. Atl had the rainbow of the Impressionists in his hands and practiced all the audacities of the Parisian School. Ruelas

15

had done a masterly self-portrait, an etching in which a monstrous insect drawn over his head was driving a gigantic sting into his skull: this represented criticism. And there were other engravings with demons in the form of succubi drinking out a poor victim's brains. The immediate future, however, did not belong to the succubi but to the violence of the rabble.

Not long after this I met Atl in the Academy. He had a studio there, and he used to visit with us in the painting rooms and the night classes. While we were copying he would entertain us, speaking in his easy, insinuating, enthusiastic tone of his travels in Europe and his stay in Rome. When he spoke of the Sistine Chapel and of Leonardo his voice took fire. The great murals! The immense frescoes of the Renaissance, incredible things, as mysterious as the pyramids of the Pharaohs, the product of a technique lost these four hundred years!

Atl was drawing muscular giants in the violent attitudes of the Sistine. We were copying models required to resemble the guilty on Doomsday.

He had already compounded his resin-dried colors, which behaved like pastels, but without their fragility. His idea, he explained, was to have colors that would do equally well in painting on paper or on canvas, or for that matter on a rock from Popocatépetl; as well for small subjects as for large ones, and on any material whatsoever, metal even, and whether sheltered or exposed. Colors that would do this would certainly be a marvel, and those he was already using, while not yet perfected, represented a long stride toward

16

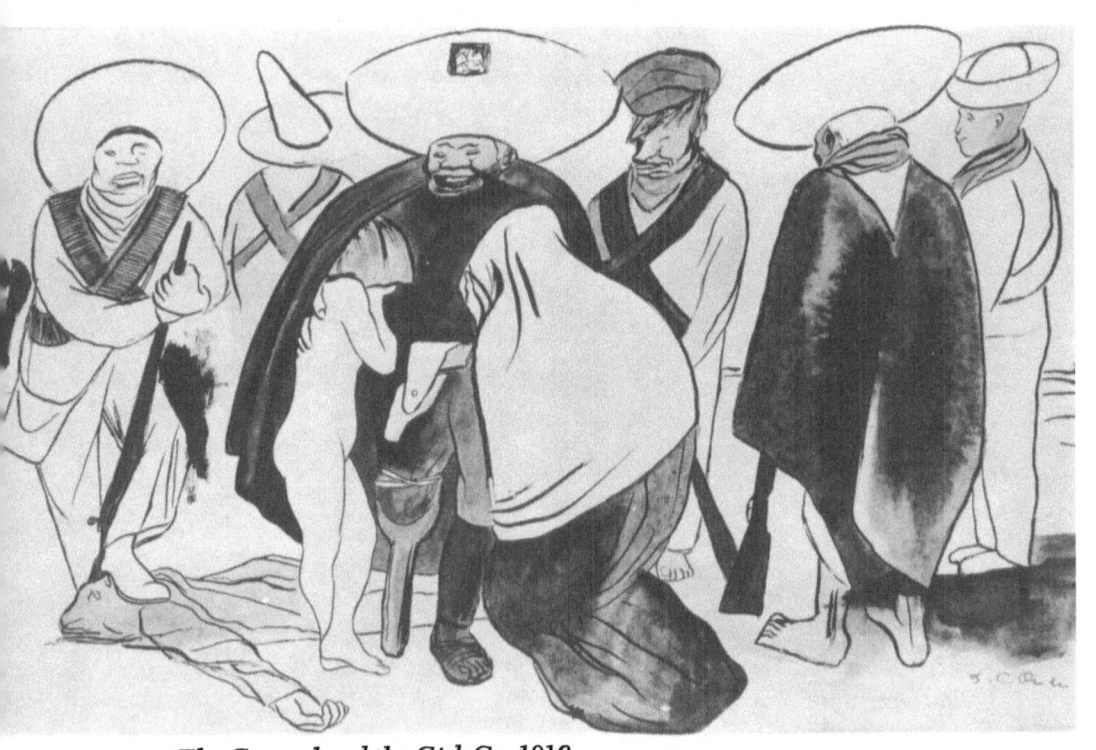

The General and the Girl. Ca. 1916.

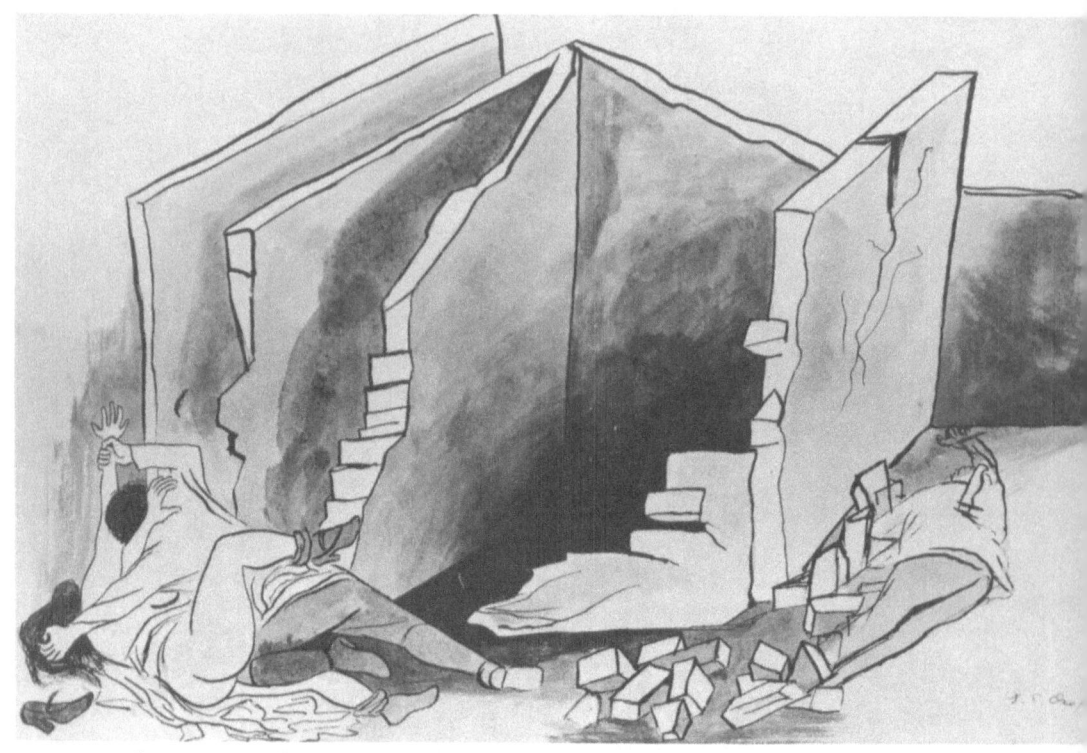

The Destroyed House. Ca. 1916.

his goal. With them he did some big pictures on canvas, paintings of volcanoes for a spacious café which stood on the south side of Sixteenth of September Street, near San Juan de Letrán. He also did a big fresco of feminine figures —nymphs or muses—carrying a garland to a portrait of Olavarrieta, a philanthropist from Puebla who had donated a valuable collection of old pictures to the Academy. The frieze was placed above these pictures when they were exhibited for the first time.

We made considerable changes in the regimen that Fabrés had left with us. Our models no longer stayed in the same position day after day. Drawing was still conscientious, but it was done rapidly, to train hand and eye. Our new exercises consisted in little by little reducing the time spent in copying from life until we could make the swiftest rough drafts, in less than a minute, and later we began to draw and paint from a model in motion. There were no longer any photographs with which to compare our efforts, and the necessary simplification of the instantaneous sketch brought out the personal style in each student.

In these night watches of apprentice painters the first signs of revolution appeared in Mexican art. The Mexican had been a poor colonial servant, incapable of creating or thinking for himself; everything had to be imported ready-made from European centers, for we were an inferior and degenerate race. They let us paint, but we had to paint the way they did in Paris, and it was the Parisian critic who would pass upon the result and pronounce the final verdict.

Architecture was refried chalets and French chateaux. The marbles and carvings in public and private buildings came from Italy.

It was inconceivable that a wretched Mexican should dream of vying with the world abroad, and so he went to that world abroad to "dedicate himself" to art, and if he ever afterward gave a thought to the backward country in which he was born it was only to beg for help in time of need, momentarily swallowing his proud "dedication," which in any case had never protected him from the suspicion of being a vulgar millionaire from the tropics.

Academic criteria held sway: "The ancients long ago reached perfection, they did everything that could be done, and nothing is left for us except to copy them and humbly imitate them. Florentine drawing with Venetian coloring. And if any painter wishes to be a modernist, let him be off to Montparnasse and there take orders."

In the nightly sessions in the Academy, as we listened to the fervent voice of that agitator Dr. Atl, we began to suspect that the whole colonial situation was nothing but a swindle foisted upon us by international traders. We too had a character, which was quite the equal of any other. We would learn what the ancients and the foreigners could teach us, but we could do as much as they, or more. It was not pride but self-confidence that moved us to this belief, a sense of our own being and our destiny.

Now for the first time the painters took stock of the country they lived in. Saturnino Herrán was already painting the

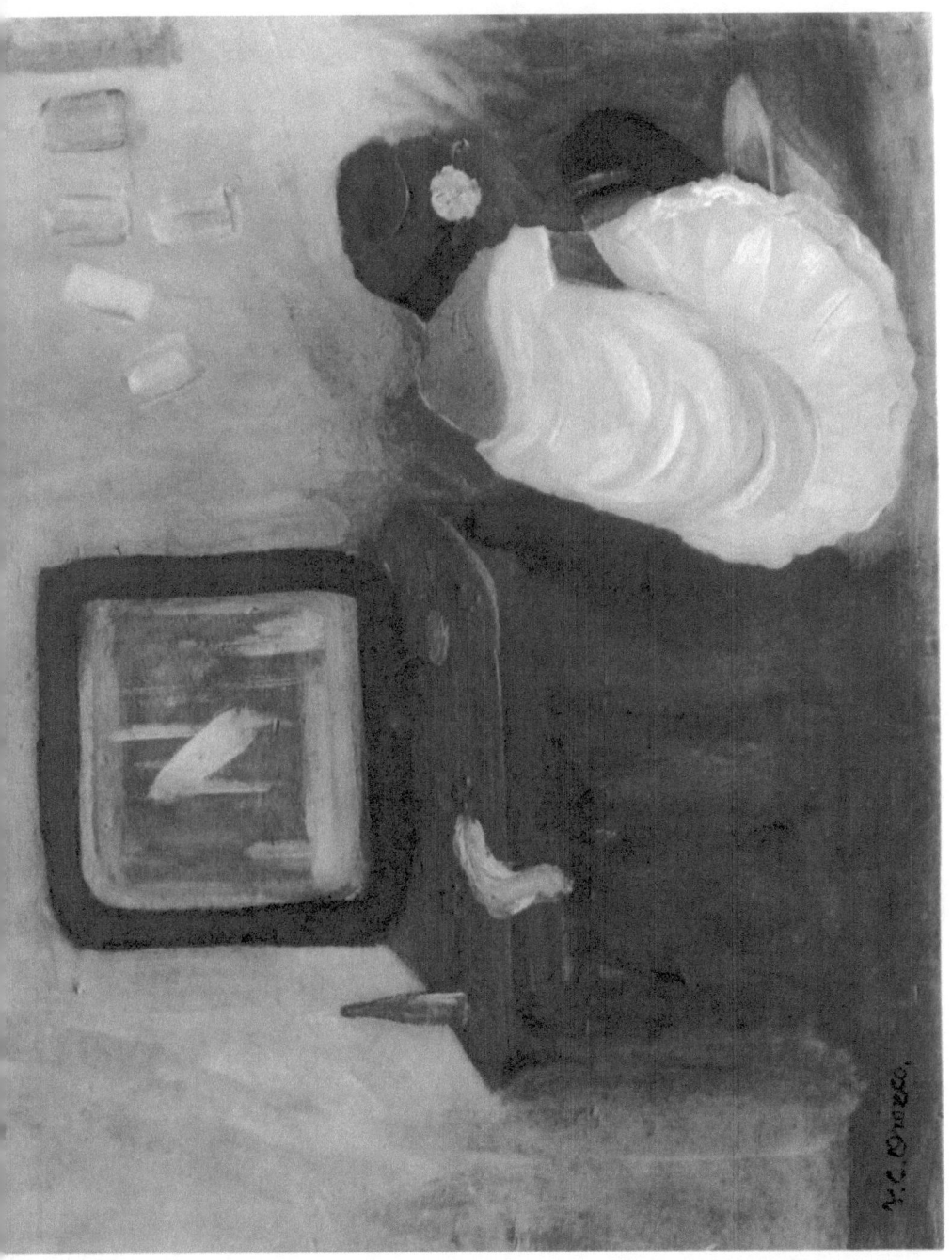

Toilette. Ca. 1912.

Creoles he knew at first hand instead of Manolas *à la* Zulo-aga. Dr. Atl went to live on Popocatépetl, and I set out to explore the wretchedest barrios in the city. On every canvas there began to appear, bit by bit, like a dawn, the Mexican landscape, and familiar forms and the colors. It was only a first and still timid step toward liberation from foreign tyr-anny, but behind it there was thorough preparation and a rigorous training.

Why must we be eternally on our knees before the Kants and the Hugos? All praise to the masters indeed, but we too could produce a Kant or a Hugo. We too could wrest iron from the bowels of the earth and fashion it into ships and machines. We could raise prodigious cities, and create na-tions, and explore the universe. Was it not from a mixture of two races that the Titans sprang?

Such was the spirit of rebellion animating our little group of apprentices (soon joined by even younger recruits), and we listened in astonishment to Dr. Atl's prophetic words: "The end of bourgeois civilization is at hand!" The end of civilization! Then civilization was bourgeois? The words were utterly new to us, though they had grown old in books.

Fabrés' successors were Don Leandro Izaguirre and Don Germán Gedovius. The first of these was the painter of the famous *Torture of Cuauhtémoc*. He belonged to the genera-tion of Mateo Herrera, when grandiose historical themes were the subjects for canvases, and it was not yet the fashion to "dedicate oneself" to art in Paris, but one went to Rome, and copied from marble the same figures that we were copy-ing from plaster.

21

Before returning to Mexico one would go on to Madrid, to make the indispensable copies of Velázquez, which one could sell to the government.

The difference between the original in the Prado Museum and the copies was no more than the difference between the sun that shines on us from heaven and a sun, in paint-shop ochre, on the filthy overalls of a bus conductor. Copy Velázquez as they would, the imitators never found out how the master of masters achieved the silvery and profound tonalities of the *Meninas*.

It was a time when painters, even the most gifted, were almost totally ignorant of the physical and chemical aspects of their art. Colors were an indecipherable mystery to them. All they knew how to do was to go to a dealer and buy so many meters of canvas and some assorted tubes of paint. How the canvas was prepared, what was in the tubes, and what chemical reactions would be produced, were questions to which they neither knew, nor attempted to learn, any answers at all. No wonder copyists in the museums rarely managed to equal the brilliant color or the solidity of the old masters.

Chapter 3 Gedovius' Studios. Rival Exhibitions in 1910. The Artistic Center. The Son of Ahuízote. The Student Strike. Raziel Cabildo.

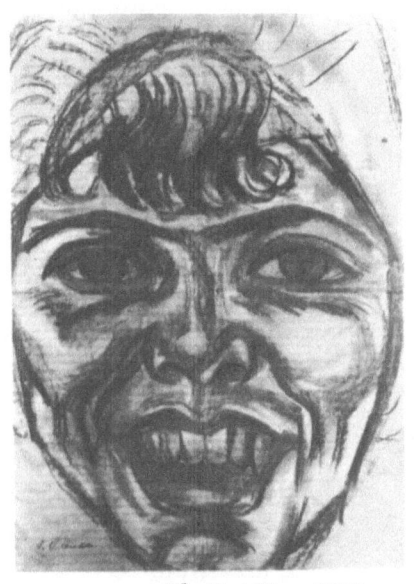

The Pug-Nose. 1934.

For the most part Gedovius' students had studied under Fabrés. But Alberto Fuster, too, joined the class on his return from Germany. Already a mature Mexican painter, he began his great triptych *The Rebels* there in the Academy. I cannot imagine where such a painting could be found today. Years later, according to the press, Fuster committed suicide in Texas. He was a brilliant painter, of grandiose conceptions and a profound knowledge of technique.

25

Another talented painter of the same period was Rubén Guzmán, who likewise disappeared.

In Gedovius' studios there was at first a great enthusiasm for work but in the course of time it lessened as discipline relaxed. The cancer of Bohemianism attacked young painters, destroying will power, talent, and lives; this was the Bohemianism we recognize in the symptoms of lank locks, laziness, filth, alcohol, and various diseases.

They worked unwillingly now, and under the platform on which the model was posing, some other model and a bold student would be making love, while the innocent master went the rounds of the easels, correcting here and advising there, without the slightest suspicion of what was going on.

At length only the petrifactions remained, that is, men and women who had entered the Academy at the age of fifteen and were to emerge past forty, without ever finally learning whether shadows were painted with lampblack or boneblack. The Academy became, and it seems that it goes on being, a warehouse of mummies and fossils.

In 1910, to celebrate the First Centenary of the Grito de Dolores, the government arranged great spectacles. One of them was an Exposition of Contemporary Spanish Painting, with the expenses defrayed by Mexico; the subsidy amounted to twenty or twenty-five thousand pesos, not counting the expensive pavilion specially erected on Avenida Juárez, across from the Hotel Regis.

Zuloaga and Sorolla, then in great vogue, were represented by numerous canvases.

26

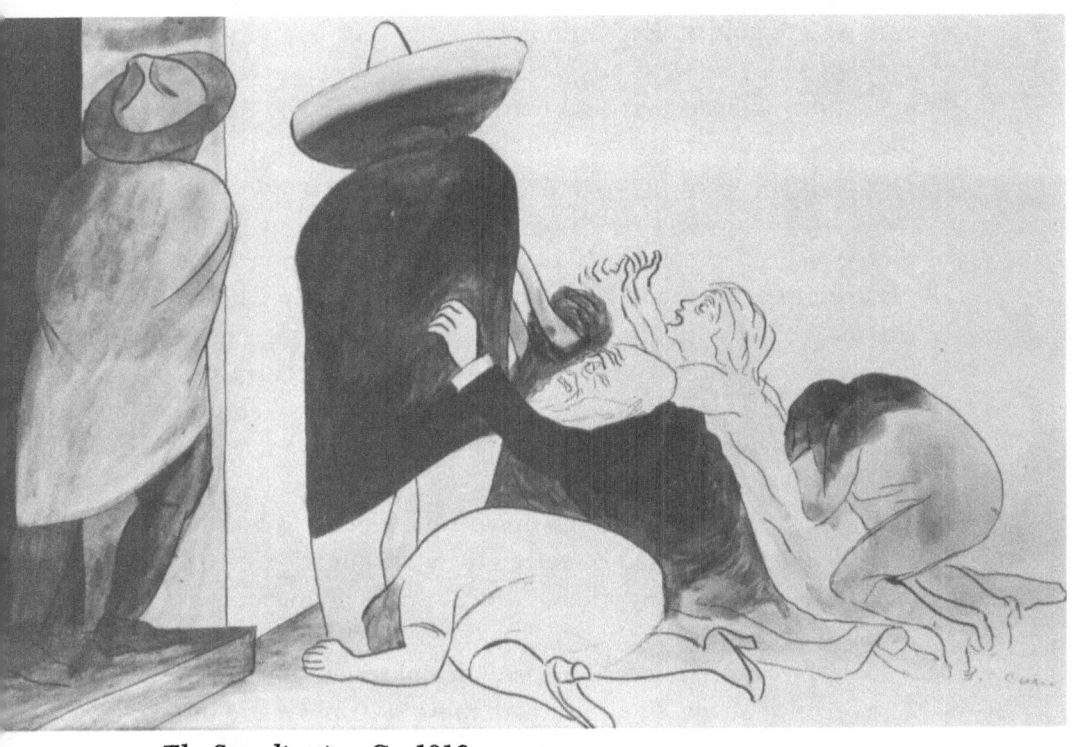

The Supplication. Ca. 1916.

We protested to the Secretariat of Instruction: it was all very well to hold an Exposition of Spanish Art, but why did they give us, the Mexicans, nothing, when it was precisely our Independence that was being celebrated? Dr. Atl, in the capacity of our leader, conducted negotiations, thanks to which we were favored with a gift of three thousand pesos for a collective showing in the Academy. Our group then consisted of some fifty painters and ten sculptors. We resolved to name the lawyer—and painter—Joaquín Clausel treasurer of the ridiculous sum, and we divided it into shares of fifty and a hundred pesos, for which each of us contracted to furnish, along with other things, two canvases, sketches, carvings, or engravings, recent and unexhibited work, within a period of two months.

There was no jury on admissions: each work was hoisted into view and accepted or rejected by acclamation of the crowd, which frequently hissed, for this was no mutual admiration society.

Our showing was an immense, an unexpected, success. The Spanish one was more formal, more stylishly made up, but ours, for all that it was improvised, was more dynamic, more varied, and more ambitious, at the same time that it was free of all pretentiousness. It filled the patio of the Academy, the corridors, and whatever halls were available. There has never been another such showing in Mexico.

Most of the young artists were exhibiting for the first time. My own contribution was a series of charcoal sketches which have since disappeared. I cannot remember what happened with them.

The adventure was not to end with this. Enthusiastic over the outcome, we accepted a proposal of Dr. Atl's: to organize a society on the spot. It would be called, we decided, the Artistic Center, and its purpose would be to secure government walls on which to do murals. Our greatest ambition would at last be realized! We rented office space on the second floor of a house in Monte de Piedad, and noisily celebrated our formal opening, eating marvelous macaroni à la Italiana, which Dr. Atl cooked in empty oil cans, and drinking rivers of beer that a brewery furnished in return for some posters we made.

We asked permission of the Secretariat of Instruction to decorate the walls of the Amphitheatre of the Preparatory School. It was granted, and we portioned out the panels and set up scaffolding.

The great Exposition of Mexican Painting had been held in September of 1910. In November we were preparing to do the murals. On the twentieth day of that month the Revolution began. There was a panic, and our projects were ruined or postponed.

We all know what followed on the triumph of the Madero Revolt, and how the government was set up. An opposition paper was one of the many "sons" of the old *Ahuizote* [a nineteenth-century satirical journal]. It was edited by Miguel Ordorica, who is today the editor of *Últimas Noticias*. A friend of mine, the newspaperman Joaquín Piña, had introduced me to him, and I went to work for him as a cartoonist. I learned how a political paper is run. Every day the assistant editors met with the editor and heatedly discussed political affairs, and the discussion gave off enough light to supply pertinent articles and cartoons. The scapegoats were, naturally, political figures of the first rank.

Jesús Luján, a friend of Ruelas', gave me a hundred pesos for the original of one of the sketches I made for the "Son." This was a bloody caricature of Madero's Staff: Sánchez Azcona, Querido Moheno, Bonilla, Gustavo Madero, Zapata, Jesús Urueta, and others.

I might equally well have gone to work for a government paper instead of the opposition, and in that case the scapegoats would have been on the other side. No artist has, or ever has had, political convictions of any sort. Those who profess to have them are not artists.

The Madero episode, a half revolution, was sheer confusion and senselessness. Except for this, everything remained what it had always been.

Rebellious ideas went on fermenting in the young painters of 1910, greatly stimulated by the general state of political disorder throughout the country.

Some of the professors, recently over from Paris, had imported a French system of teaching drawing, the "Pillet System," somewhat worse than copying engravings and plaster casts. This finally broke the patience of the students, who went on a strike which lasted for two years, from 1911 to 1913. Antonio Rivas Mercado, architect, constructor of the Monument of Independence and director of the Academy, was stoned by a mob of students, and this was the first time

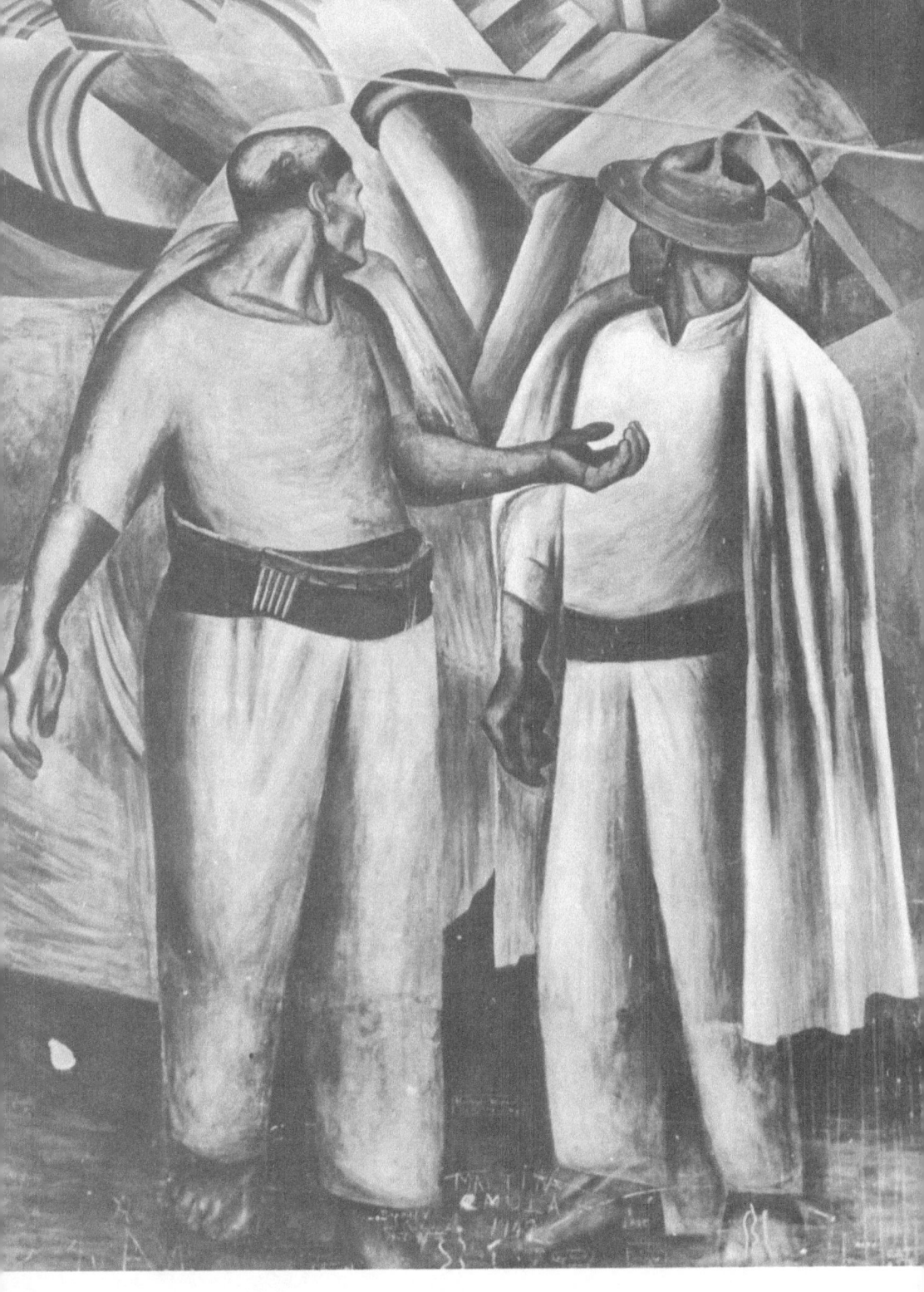

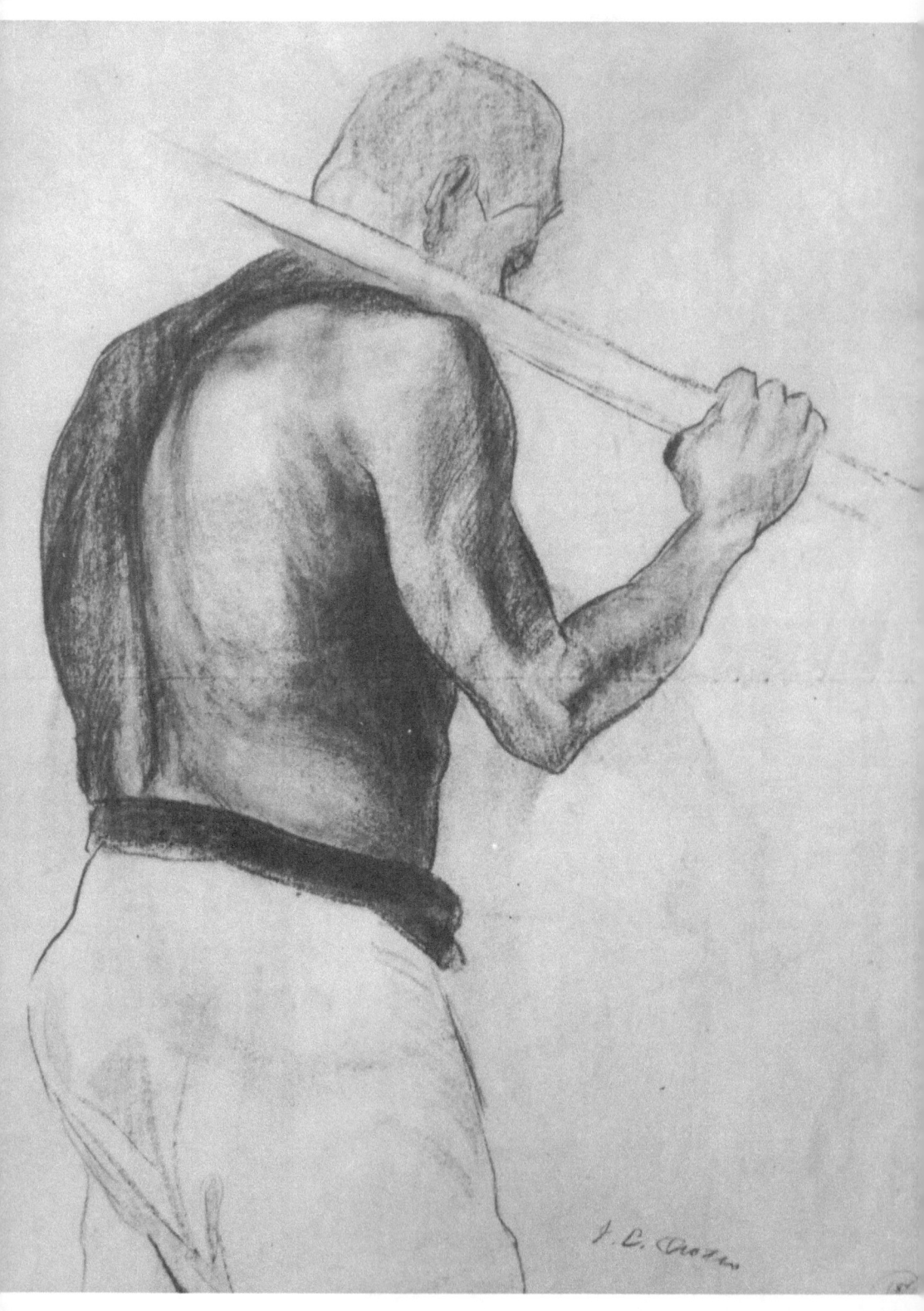

that Alfaro Siqueiros and Ignacio Asúnsolo went to jail. The students demanded that Rivas Mercado and the "Pillet" professors be dismissed, and the curriculum radically revised.

Dr. Atl had gone off to Europe, and the leader of the movement was Raziel Cabildo, the most cultivated and even-tempered of companions.

Raziel was a romantic poet who had come to the Academy to study painting. He was a gentle fellow and an excellent friend, incapable of the least act of disloyalty. Under such titles as "Azul," he published little literary journals which would not run beyond the second or third numbers.

Another dear friend was Ramón López, a man, like Raziel, of snow-white soul and the purest of thoughts. They too were Bohemians but theirs was the poetical and idealistic Bohemia of Rodolfo bidding Mimí a last farewell. Ramón López wore a flowing black beard and a great broad-brimmed hat. He painted slowly—figures and landscapes which I remembered years later when I came to know the work of Cézanne, but which were saturated with a melancholy absent in Cézanne, though they were constructed quite as solidly as the works of the French master. Ramón López did not know Cézanne, not even in reproductions. He died in 1914.

It was Raziel, naturally, who edited the manifestos against the Academy. Their language had nothing incendiary about it but was as suave and harmonious as that of Rubén Darío. Into the shock brigade went the illiterates:

33

Peasant with a Hoe. Ca. 1926.

Asúnsolo, Fernández Urbina, Alfaro Siqueiros, the Labrador brothers (now powerful bankers on Isabel la Católica Street), José de Jesús Ibarra (today a journalist), Luis G. Serrano, Romano Guillemín, and Miguel Angel Fernández.

Since the strike led to no conclusion, we would foregather in the local bars.

Raziel, Ramón López, and Francisco de la Torre would end by weeping disconsolately over their tequila, as they listened to Raziel's dolorous verses to a dancer, and Ramón López' "Sad Tolling of the Bells" or his gloomy songs with their invocation to "Inhuman Death."

34

Chapter 4

Ramos Martínez. Bar-bizon in Santa Anita. My Studio on Illescas. My Wartime Exploits. Victoriano Huerta. Gambling Halls and Conscription. The Theatre María Tepache.

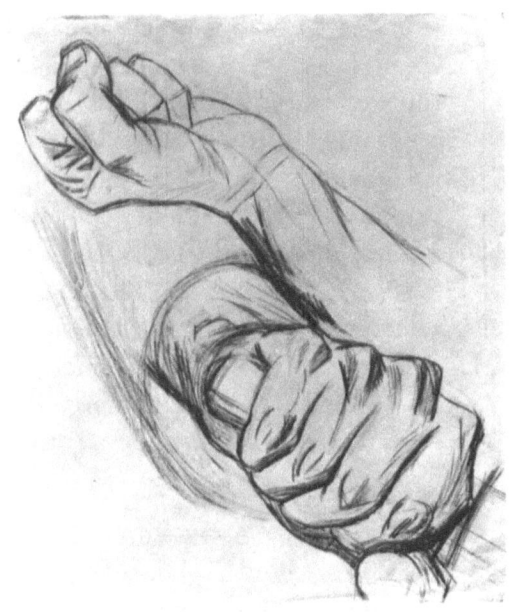

Study of Hidalgo's Hands. 1938.

In 1911 or 1912 Alfredo Ramos Martínez was just back from Paris. We knew his *Spring,* in which four or five aristocratic girls are shown in garments of vaporous texture and delicate colors, amidst an inundation of flowers, ribbons, and laces, and the whole picture is bathed in a perfume-laden atmosphere.

Painters who went to Europe on scholarships were required to send pictures home to Mexico every year, for group showings. So we

37

came to know the Balearic Islands, Montenegro, Rivera's *The House at the Bridge*, Ramos Martínez' own works, and those of Angel Zárraga, Téllez Toledo, and Goitia.

Ramos Martínez launched his candidacy for director of the Academy and solicited the support of the strikers, promising to slay the academic monster and inaugurate reforms in the plan of studies. He showed us a rich collection of iridescent silk garments his models had worn for *Spring*. He talked at great length of Renoir, Matisse, Claude Monet, Pissarro; in a word, the French Impressionists and the village they had made so famous: Barbizon. The young painters succumbed, once for all, to the Parisian witchery of *Spring*.

Ramos Martínez became director, and the first thing he did was to found a school of open-air painting in Santa Anita and give it the pompous name of "Barbizon." It was as if he had founded a Santa Anita on the Seine—close to Paris, within a few paces of the Eiffel Tower, complete with carriers, pulque, country dandies, enchiladas, huaraches, knife thrusts, and all.

This is not to condemn his innovation; on the contrary, it was a natural reaction against an Academy already in a state of decomposition. The good old academic methods, based upon order and discipline, had disappeared, leaving only ineptitude and routine behind. What was bad in the change was the consequences, of which we shall speak later.

So much open air was little to my taste, and I broke with the group. I opened a studio in Illescas Street, now called

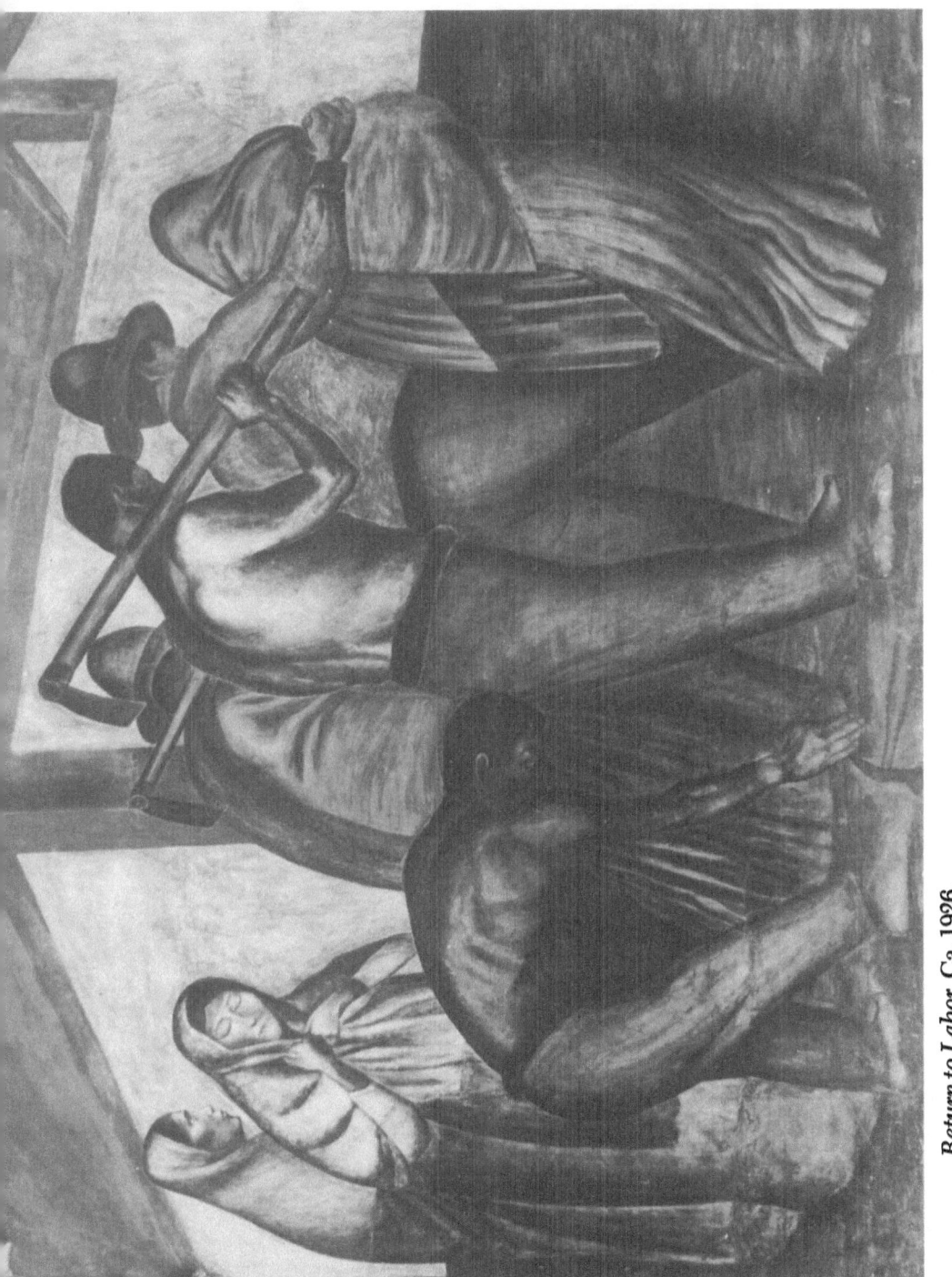

Return to Labor. Ca. 1926.

Pedro Ascencio, in a neighborhood plagued with luxurious houses of the most magnificent notoriety, which sheltered "embassies" from France, Africa, the Caribbean, and North and Central America.

Out in the open air the Barbizonians were painting very pretty landscapes, with the requisite violets for the shadows and Nile green for the skies, but I preferred black and the colors exiled from Impressionist palettes. Instead of red and yellow twilight, I painted the pestilent shadows of closed rooms, and instead of the Indian male, drunken ladies and gentlemen.

My studio was frequented by the most radiant of goddesses. It enchanted them to appear in my pictures and they were happy to carry these away after posing for them.

I played no part in the Revolution, I came to no harm, and I ran no danger at all. To me the Revolution was the gayest and most diverting of carnivals, that is, of what I take carnivals to be, for I have never seen one. The great leaders I knew only by sight, from seeing them parade through the streets at the head of their troops, accompanied by their staff officers. It was consequently very funny to read the many articles that American papers published about my wartime adventures. A headline in one San Francisco daily ran, "The Bare-Footed Soldier of the Revolution." Another paper gave the most minute details of my differences with Carranza, who, it seems, was persecuting me implacably for satirical attacks upon him. The most fantastic report of all was a dramatic account of how I had lost my left hand while throwing bombs in a terrible encounter between Villistas and Zapatistas. The truth of the matter is that I lost my hand when a child, playing with powder: it was an accident in no way out of the ordinary. Other stories had me carrying the banner of the Indian Cause, and these were accompanied by a picture of my person in which I could recognize a Tarahumara. I have never espoused the Cause of the Indians, or thrown bombs, or even, though another paper reported it, been shot on three separate occasions.

The "Tragic Tenth," or as some called it the "Magic Tenth," was indeed terrible, but I was neither in the citadel at the time nor in the neighborhood. Cunning General Victoriano Huerta launched the Maderist battalions against the cannon and machine guns with which the fortress bristled, and the poor Maderists fell like so many flies under a flit gun. Leaving them to dispose of General Reyes, Don Victoriano had Madero and Pino Suárez executed. With General Felix Díaz he did not bother, for Díaz was as inoffensive as a butterfly. One by one he disposed of his remaining adversaries. There is no doubt that he was a monster, but in this he was no different from other Victoriano Huertas whose exploits fill the pages of history. In like fashion others have assassinated fathers, brothers, or friends on their way to a throne. Afterwards they have persuaded the Pope to crown them and Leonardo da Vinci to do an equestrian statue of them.

Many are the fine ladies who have sent the king, their consort, to slaughter as if he were a turkey for their dinner; and

afterwards they seated themselves upon the throne and surrounded themselves with favorites, whose lives hung by a
thread. Victoriano Huerta dispensed with having the Pope
crown him, but then neither did he order an equestrian
statue—which would have afforded a magnificent opportunity to the sculptors Fernández Urbina, Domínguez Bello,
or Nacho Asúnsolo. Instead of a sword they could have put
a bottle of cognac in his right hand.

If princes, dukes, kings, and emperors have first assassinated the relatives who blocked their road to power, and
then commissioned sculptors to raise equestrian statues to
them in plazas and streets, there could be no great difficulty
in our having a Victoriano Huerta Avenue. It is at least
euphonious. History is subject to truly surprising and dis-
concerting corrections.

To make fiscal ends meet, Don Victoriano set up gambling houses throughout the city. There were more of these
than saloons and pulque bars, one or two in every block.
Some of them were luxurious places in which to fleece the
bourgeois, and others, which we might call proletarian,
were places where workers and peasants could lose as little
as five centavos a throw. At the time there were neither labor unions nor arbitration boards, since otherwise the workers would have stayed out on strike against the gambling
establishments until these were turned over to them.

By night the city was fantastic. Countless haunts of dis-
sipation were crowded with women of easy morals and offi-

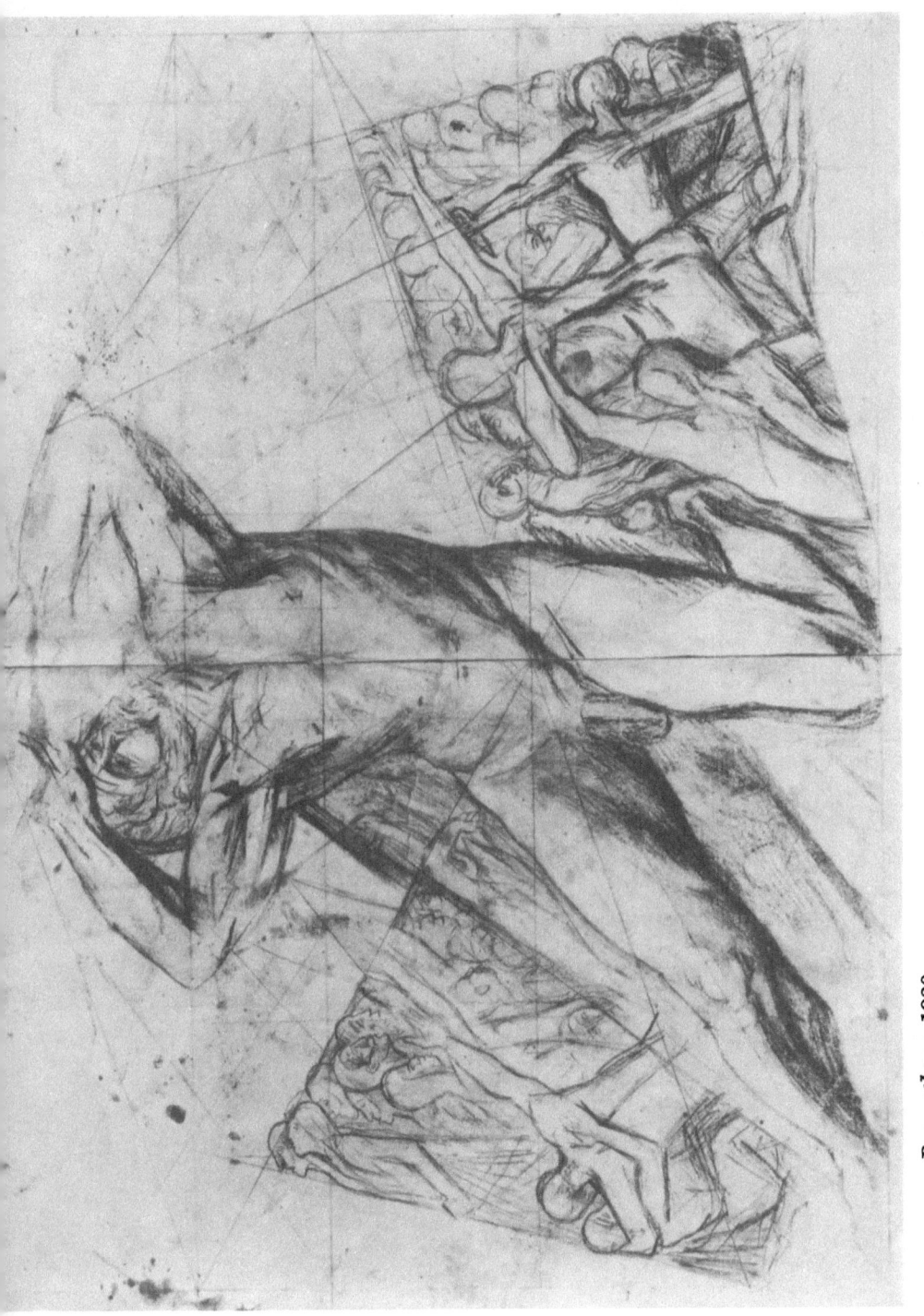

Prometheus. 1930.

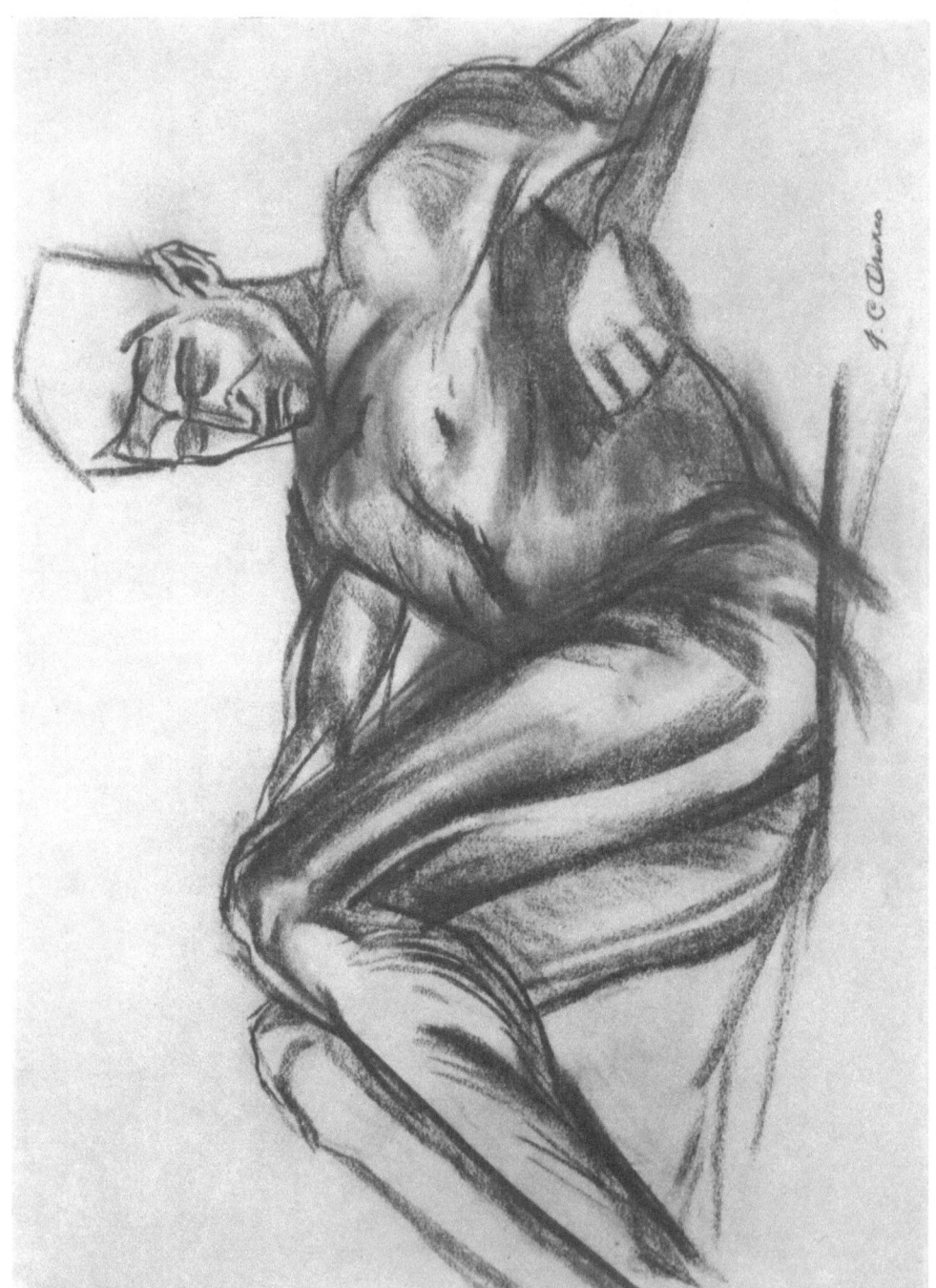

Man Reclining. 1939.

cers from Huerta's army. There were eighteen-year-old captains and twenty-five-year-old colonels.

Recruiting under the usurper was a sort of draft. At best, night hawks would find themselves in a block which the police had suddenly roped off at both ends, and all the males from among them would be carted away. I myself fell into these traps a number of times, but I was always released on the spot because of my missing hand. At other times they would suddenly close a bar or some such place, and the able-bodied customers would be herded into the army. In great warlike nations the same practice is followed, but to the letter, for the names of the new recruits are at least set down in a book.

One of the most frequented spots in Huertist times was the Theatre María Guerrero, or as it was also called, María Tepache, in the Peralvillo District. These were the best days of the actors Beristáin and Acevedo, who created a unique genre. Their audience was utterly hybrid: the filthiest scum of the city mixed with intellectuals and artists, with army officers, bureaucrats, politicians, and even secretaries of state. They conducted themselves worse than at bullfights; they pushed their way into the very performances, taking the most familiar tone with the actors and actresses, and insulting one another and making such changes in the dialogue that no two performances were alike. From the gallery above, all sorts of missiles fell onto the heads of those in the orchestra seats—spit, pulque, and even worse liquids; and sometimes the drunks themselves came tumbling down

45

upon those below. It is easy to imagine the effects that actors and audience achieved between them. The fury of the rabble broke out in a dense and sickening atmosphere, and the spectacles were often of the most alarming sort. Yet for all this there was much wit, and telling characterization. Beristáin and Acevedo were wonderfully good at "taking off" marijuana addicts, convicts, and policemen. The "actresses" were all of them terribly old and deformed.

Later the genre degenerated (this is no paradox) and turned political—and suitable for families. It became a tourist attraction. A chorus was introduced into it, Tehuanas with their cups of chocolate, black-suited dandies from the villages, with sentimental and vulgar songs done by singers from Los Angeles and San Antonio, Texas, things, all of them, insupportable and in the worst possible taste, but dear to the hearts of decent families from apartment, or as they were formerly called, neighborhood, houses. Retribution was not long deferred. It all ended in the cinema and the horrible radio, with its announcers, loud speakers, and interminable idiocy.

I don't know whether this is the end of bourgeois civilization, of which so much is prophesied, or the beginning of a new civilization. In either case it is detestable.

Chapter 5

Dr. Atl Returns. Handing Out Money. The House of the World Worker. Orizaba. Storming and Sacking Churches. Red Battalions. *The Vanguard.*

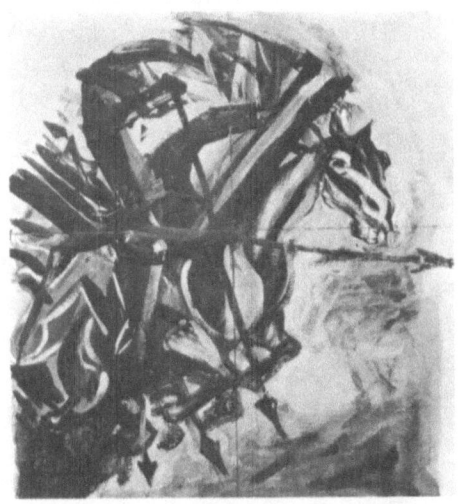

Horses and Spears in Space. 1939.

The Revolution followed its course. Various leaders rose against Victoriano Huerta, followed by their twenty thousand generals and these in turn by their many thousands of soldiers and the wives and children of the latter, that is, by the people *en masse*.

The most prominent of the leaders were Carranza, Villa, and Obregón in the north and Zapata in the south. Carranza wanted to lead them all. Villa would not be led, nor Zapata

49

either. The four of them fought among themselves, not, however, without first having disposed of Victoriano Huerta. Obregón then drove Villa off the scene after some terrific battles. The cannonading was frightful and irresistible. Zapata, meanwhile, was indomitable, but hidden away in his mountains.

Fresh from campaigning against Huerta in the European press, Dr. Atl, I learned, was back in Mexico disguised as an Italian, without his beard and speaking Italian exclusively.

When Obregón and Villa were still fighting, Villa descended upon Mexico City and Obregón prepared to effect a strategic evacuation. With lines of communication cut, the inhabitants of the city were brought close to starvation, work was at a standstill, there was misery everywhere. Obregón therefore ordered hundreds of thousands of pesos to be distributed, in the form of paper money that rolled off the plates faster than newspapers from a rotary press, but without any silver behind it. Each of the generals printed his own money.

Various persons were commissioned to do the distributing, among them Atl, who in his turn commissioned us, his former companions, to aid him in the task. Once more the Academy became the headquarters of the painters, and it was from there that we set out one morning, each of us carrying thick packets of ten- and twenty-peso notes, fresh from the factory. I myself headed toward Coyoacán and amused myself for several hours in handing out money to people who at first paid no attention, thinking it was leaflets.

But when they saw that it actually was money, they flung themselves upon me and, with noise of the incredible happening, hundreds came running to demand their share. I fled toward the Plaza of Coyoacán to catch a trolley car. Behind me the crowd rushed along, but this, it happened, was because the Zapatistas were on their way to the city, from the south. I managed to get aboard a car that was just starting. The motorman jammed the control all the way over and within a few minutes we had reached the city and were entering the Zócalo at top speed.

Dr. Atl was in full revolutionary career on the side of Obregón. Having to leave within a few days, he was getting ready to join in the retreat toward Vera Cruz.

In the House of the World Worker the workers were divided in opinion as to which side to take, the Villista or the Carrancista. They had assembled to make their decision, and the discussion had been a long and stormy one when Dr. Atl appeared among them and with his eloquence completely carried them over onto the Carrancista side.

Railway convoys were organized and the whole House of the World Worker set out *en masse* for Orizaba. On a freight train most of the press, the implements, and the accessories of *El Imparcial* were shipped to this same city, and in another train we went along—Dr. Atl, some of us painters, and our friends and relatives.

The first order of business in Orizaba was to invade and sack the churches. That of Los Dolores was emptied, to clear the nave for a couple of plane presses, several linotype machines, and the apparatus of an engraving shop. It was our purpose to issue a revolutionary newspaper under the title of *The Vanguard,* and the adjoining parish house was turned into editorial rooms.

The Church of El Carmen, likewise taken over, was turned into a shelter for the World Worker. Saints, confessionals, and altars we chopped into kindling for the women to do their cooking with, and we ourselves appropriated the ornaments of altar and clergy alike. We left the scene of pillage, all of us, decorated with rosaries, medallions, and scapularies.

In still another of the emptied churches we set up other presses and linotype machines for a paper the workers were to edit. These workers, organized into the first "red" battalions to appear in Mexico, later acquitted themselves brilliantly in battle with the Villistas.

While the presses of *The Vanguard* were being readied, Dr. Atl would occupy the pulpit and preach the ideals of the Constitutional Revolution, developing the thousand and one projects that he had for making over everything: art, science, journalism, literature, and so on.

The Vanguard soon made its appearance. Dr. Atl was editor-in-chief; Raziel Cabildo, managing editor; Elodia Ramírez was in charge of the stenographers; the subeditors were Juan Manuel Giffard, Manuel Becerra Acosta, Francisco Valladares, Luis Castillo Ledón and Rafael Aveleyra; the draftsmen, Miguel Angel Fernández and Romano Guil-

52

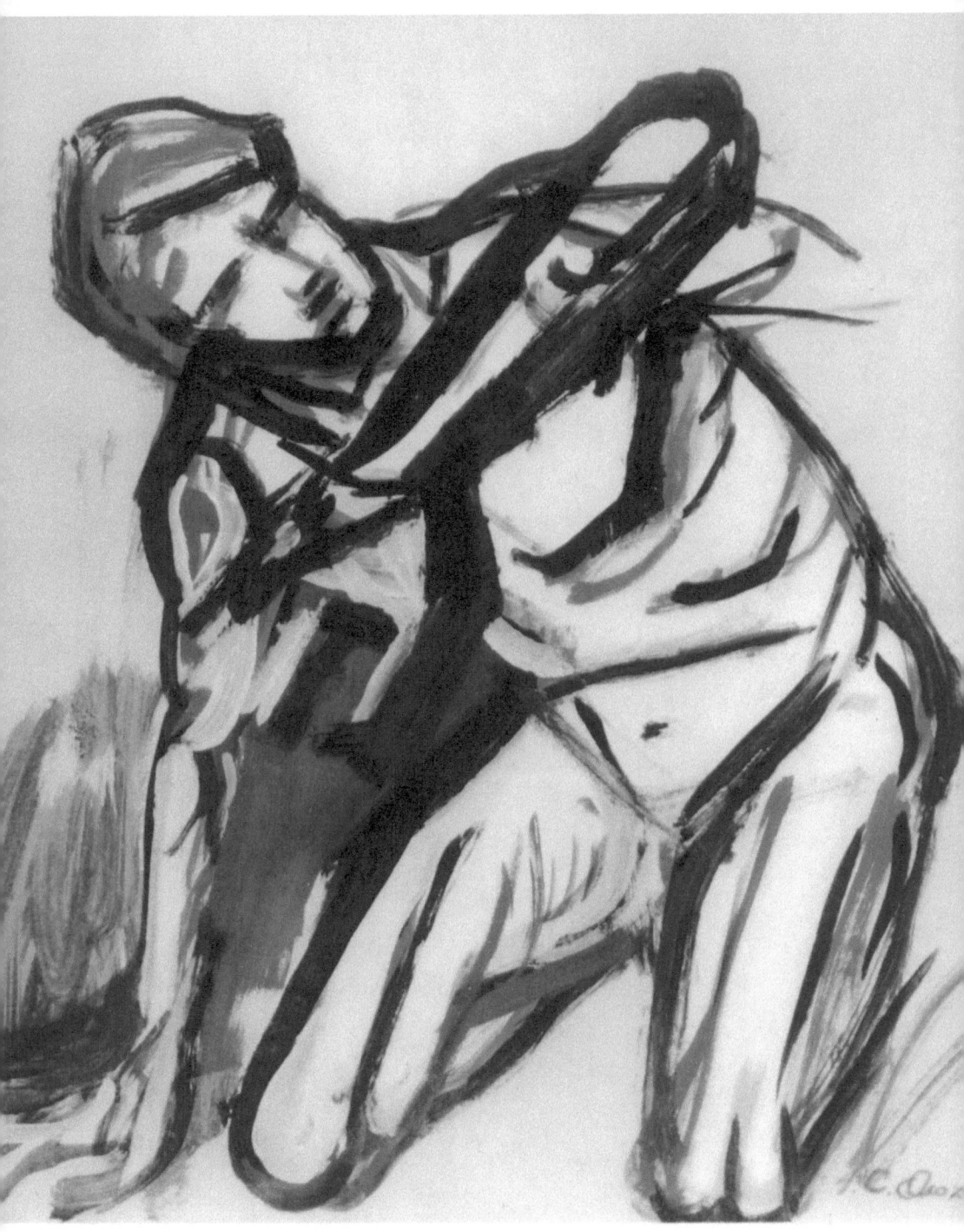

Kneeling Man. 1942.

lemín; the engraver, Tostado; the consultant on architecture, Francisco Centeno; and the caricaturist, Clemente Orozco. To fold and assemble the sheets of the paper we had the daughters of the group, all of them beautiful and one among them, Josefina Rafael, exquisitely so. Alfaro Siqueiros and Francisco Valladares were sent to represent *The Vanguard* at the front, where General Diéguez was fighting the Villistas in Jalisco.

Life in Orizaba was of the most agreeable and entertaining character. We worked enthusiastically. The town was lively. There was music on all sides. Luis Castillo Ledón spent his mornings in training his mustachios to flare à la Kaiser Wilhelm, and his afternoon in writing articles. Dr. Atl, with rifle and cartridge belt, would be off to Vera Cruz to visit Obregón on the field of battle and collect money for our whole establishment; all the while conducting a ferocious political controversy with the engineer Félix P. Palavicini and resolving a thousand problems and still having time left over in which to write editorials, and books, and even poems, without once neglecting his magnificent collection of butterflies. Raziel Cabildo, with Elodia Ramírez' help, would be organizing the work of the editorial rooms; Manuel Becerra Acosta (Julio the Off-Color) was busy turning Orizaba off-color with his satires; and Fernández and Romano Guillemín did the illumined posters that advertised *The Vanguard*. Francisco Centeno wrote love letters that never reached the hands of the beloved; and I did handbills and furious anticlerical caricatures.

We lived together in a building we had expropriated; it

53

had been a convent and consequently was large enough to house both families and single men. We called it the Thicket.

But the world was torn apart around us. Troop convoys passed on their way to slaughter. Trains were blown up. In the portals of churches wretched Zapatist peasants, who had fallen prisoners to the Carrancistas, were summarily shot down. People grew used to killing, to the most pitiless egotism, to the glutting of the sensibilities, to naked bestiality. Little towns were stormed and subjected to every sort of excess. Trains back from the battlefield unloaded their cargoes in the station in Orizaba: the wounded; the tired; exhausted, mutilated soldiers, sweating and tatterdemalion.

In the world of politics it was the same, war without quarter, struggle for power and wealth. Factions and subfactions were past counting, the thirst for vengeance insatiable. And underneath it all, subterranean intrigues went on among the friends of today and the enemies of tomorrow, resolved, when the time came, upon mutual extermination.

Farce, drama, barbarity. Buffoons and dwarfs trailing along after the gentlemen of noose and dagger, in conference with smiling procuresses. Insolent leaders, inflamed with alcohol, taking whatever they wanted at pistol point.

By night in dark streets the sound of gunplay, followed by screams, blasphemies, and vile insults. Breaking windows, sharp blows, cries of pain, and shots again.

A parade of stretchers with the wounded in bloody rags, and all at once the savage pealing of bells and a thunder of rifle fire. Drums and cornets in a reveille drowned out by the

54

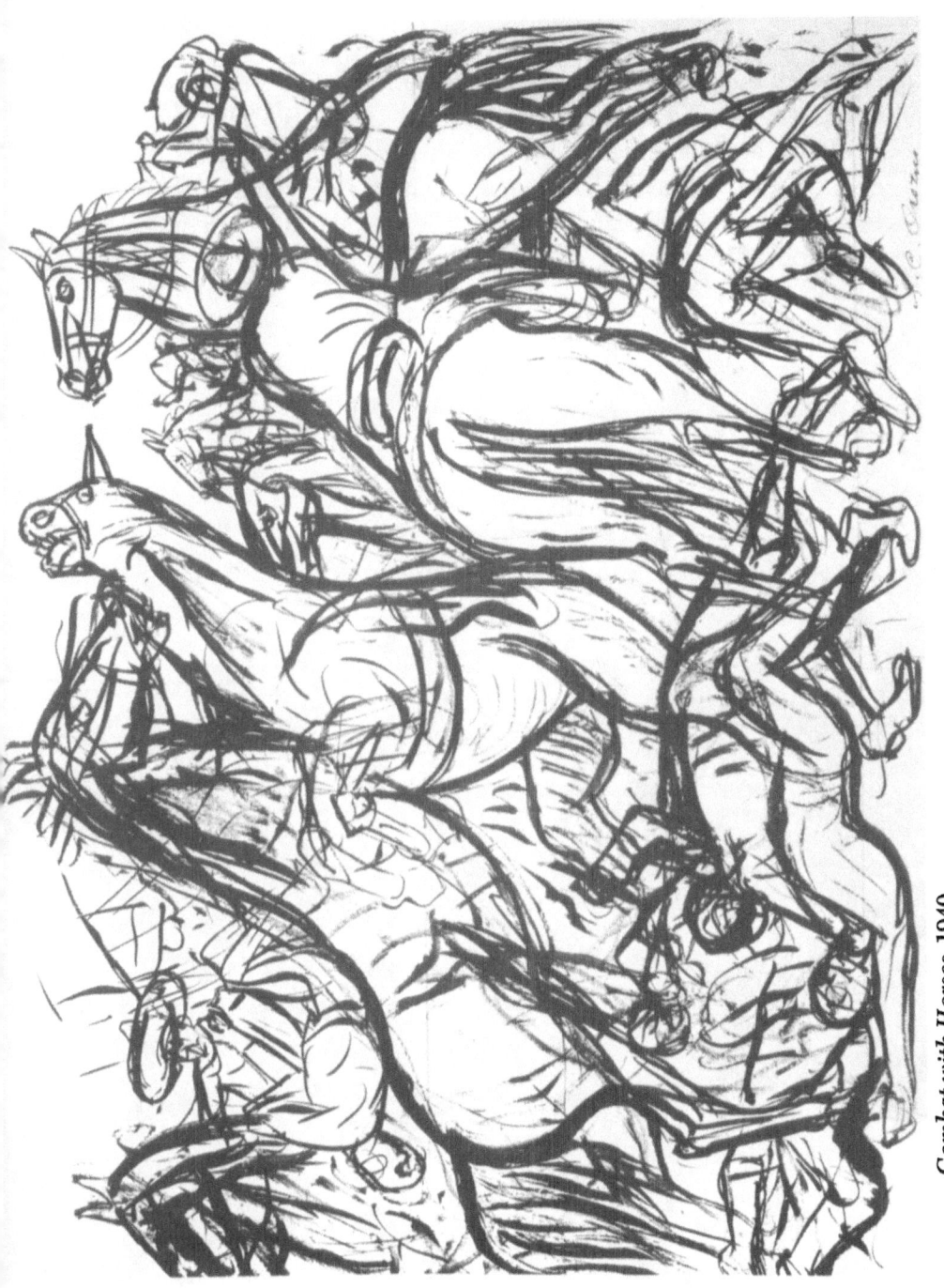

Combat with Horses. 1940.

cries of the crowd. Viva Obregón! Death to Villa! Viva Carranza! "La Cucaracha" accompanied by firing. The triumphs at Trinidad and Celaya were celebrated scandalously, and meanwhile the poor Zapatistas who had fallen prisoners were brutally beaten by the Carrancist crowd out in front of the church.

Chapter 6 Customs Officers in Laredo, Texas. San Francisco, California. Fernando G. Galván and Company. The League of Nations. Expulsion from Canada.

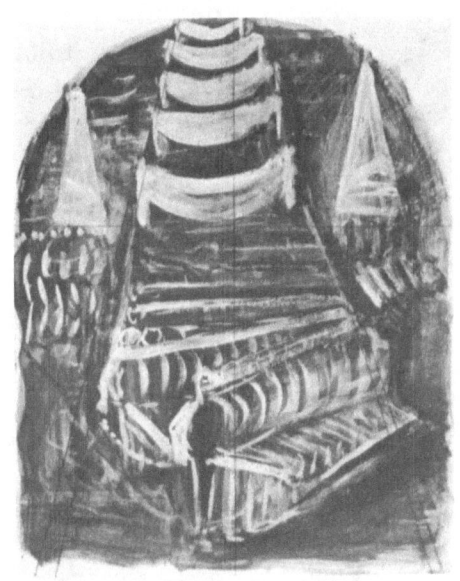

The Regimentation of the Masses. 1939.

*I*n 1917, finding the atmosphere in Mexico unfavorable to art and wishing to know the United States, I resolved to go North. I made a bundle of whatever paintings were left in my studio in Illescas, some hundred in all, and set out.

In Laredo, Texas, I was detained in the Customs and my baggage was inspected. My pictures, scattered through the office in an "official" showing, were minutely examined by the Customs officers. After this some sixty of them

59

were set aside and destroyed. I was given to understand that it was against the law to bring immoral drawings into the United States. The pictures were far from immoral, there was nothing shameless about them, there weren't even any nudes, but the officials were firm in the conviction that they were protecting the purity and innocence of North America from stain, or else that domestic concupiscence was in sufficient supply, without any need to be augmented from abroad. At first I was too dumbfounded to utter a word, but then when I did protest furiously it was of no avail, and I sadly continued on my way to San Francisco.

In that magnificent city Joaquín Piña hospitably received me, and introduced me to Fernando R. Galván. Another carnival began, but this time to the sound of the First World War.

San Francisco was an animated place. On all sides officers and soldiers glittered in their brilliant uniforms; I saw sailors, the prettiest of nurses, fat-jowled business men making colossal fortunes, and Chinese girls in their embroidered pantaloons and characteristic tunics.

The city had risen anew from its ashes after an earthquake and fire that almost totally destroyed it in 1906 or 1907, and it stood there proudly on one of the two peninsulas that form the Golden Gate and the incomparable bay —in a unique geographical position, one of the most beautiful settings in the world, which only the pen of a Balzac or a Maupassant could describe, pausing, as they used to do, and interrupting action and dialogue, in order to add the masterly details of landscapes in which their characters moved. These were the long passages that I always skipped, for I was impatient to follow the principal characters in their adventures.

We heard the song "Over There" at all hours. The air was thick with it. We breathed it, we smelled it. It seeped into stone façade and the asphalt of the streets. We ate it, like the "hot cakes" and the "scrambled eggs."

Tattooed, herculean sailors, in single file, each with his hands on the shoulders of the man in front of him, wound and danced in the streets, singing "Over There."

Everywhere were great army tents, housing buffets worthy of a formal reception in an embassy and presided over by fine ladies from the social world. The buffets were for the tired soldiers and sailors, for whom likewise were padded chairs and couches, newspapers, magazines, cigars, cigarettes, tobacco, matches, stamps, postcards, shoe-shine stands, and a countless lot of such necessary things.

The Devil, for the moment, was the Kaiser, the Number One Enemy of Democracy, and everywhere his effigy was to be encountered, with his aggressive mustachios and his helmet. Big placards expressed the general sentiment, "To Hell with the Kaiser."

Mexicans swarmed through San Francisco, so that often pure Spanish was to be heard in the streets. To the numbers of the Mexicans native to California were added the exiles, victims of the Carrancista régime, or malcontents, or simply those who had come up from Sonora or Sinaloa to escape the vexation of civil war.

Galván and I made friends and resolved to join forces in some endeavor. Our first idea was for me to paint some pictures and him to sell them. He asked me for the paintings I had brought along, and was disappointed. He said that they were absolutely lacking in commercial value. So we discarded them.

To go into business and have a place to live in we needed a house, and after some search we found on Mission Street an immense barracks of a room which had been a workshop. Galván being something of a carpenter, we used cheap materials to divide the place into a couple of bedrooms, a bath, a living room, a dining room, a kitchen, an office, a studio, and a carpenter shop. We painted it green on the outside, and in enormous yellow letters, legible for miles, we raised our sign: FERNANDO R. GALVAN & COMPANY. I, all by myself, was the "Company."

We had neither furniture nor money, but in North America you can buy anything on credit, provided you have a telephone, which seems to constitute a guarantee of the most unimpeachable sort. We applied for a telephone, which brought in its train furniture, bed linen, a typewriter, an easel, and abundant painter's supplies.

Galván sallied out in search of "orders" and got a good one: to do hand-painted announcements of pictures for a couple of movie houses; but no such "painting by hand" was actually called for, only a simple deception: the colored lithographs that they gave us as models could be pasted onto cardboard and given three or four brush strokes of oil paint.

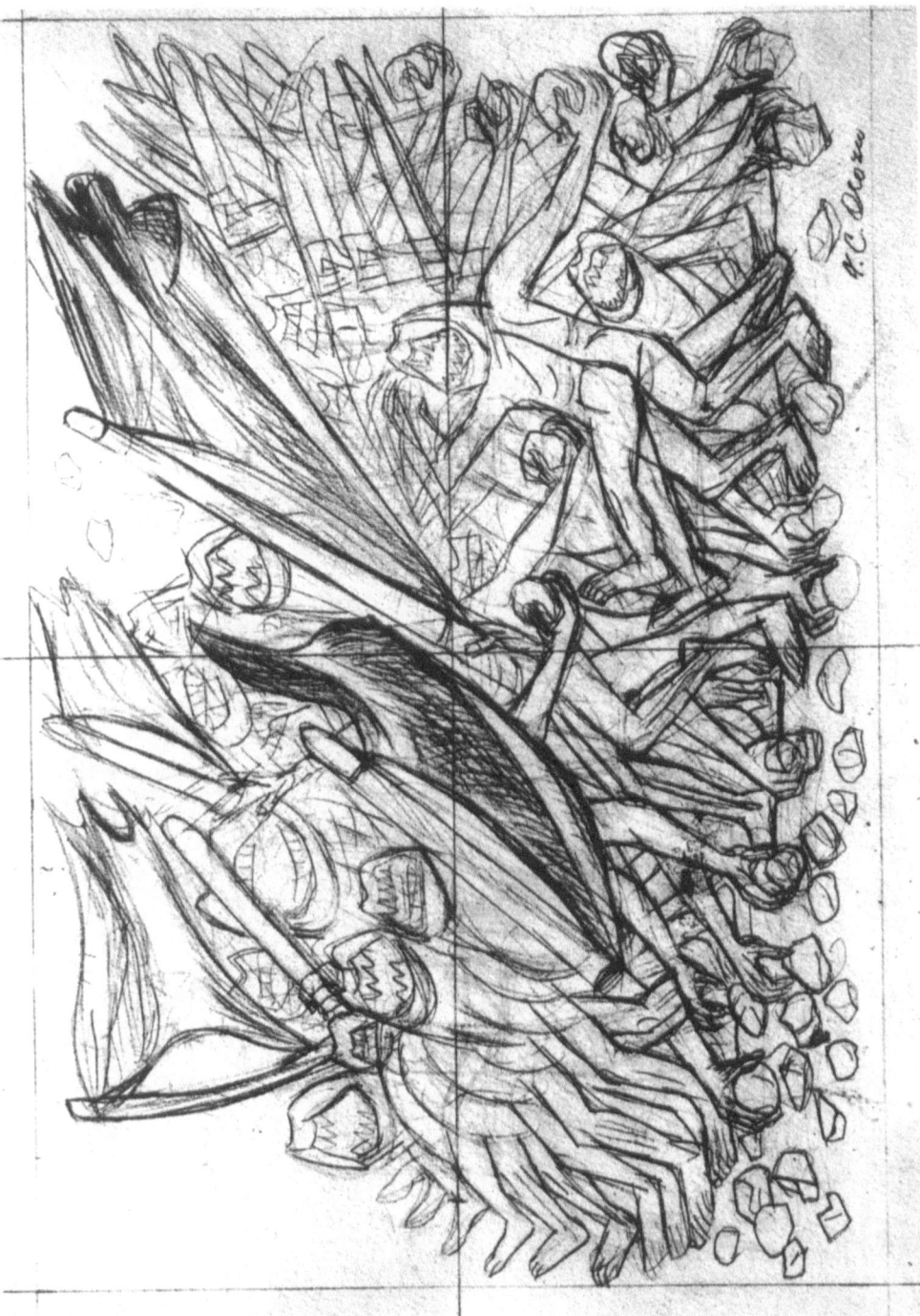

The Masses. 1940.

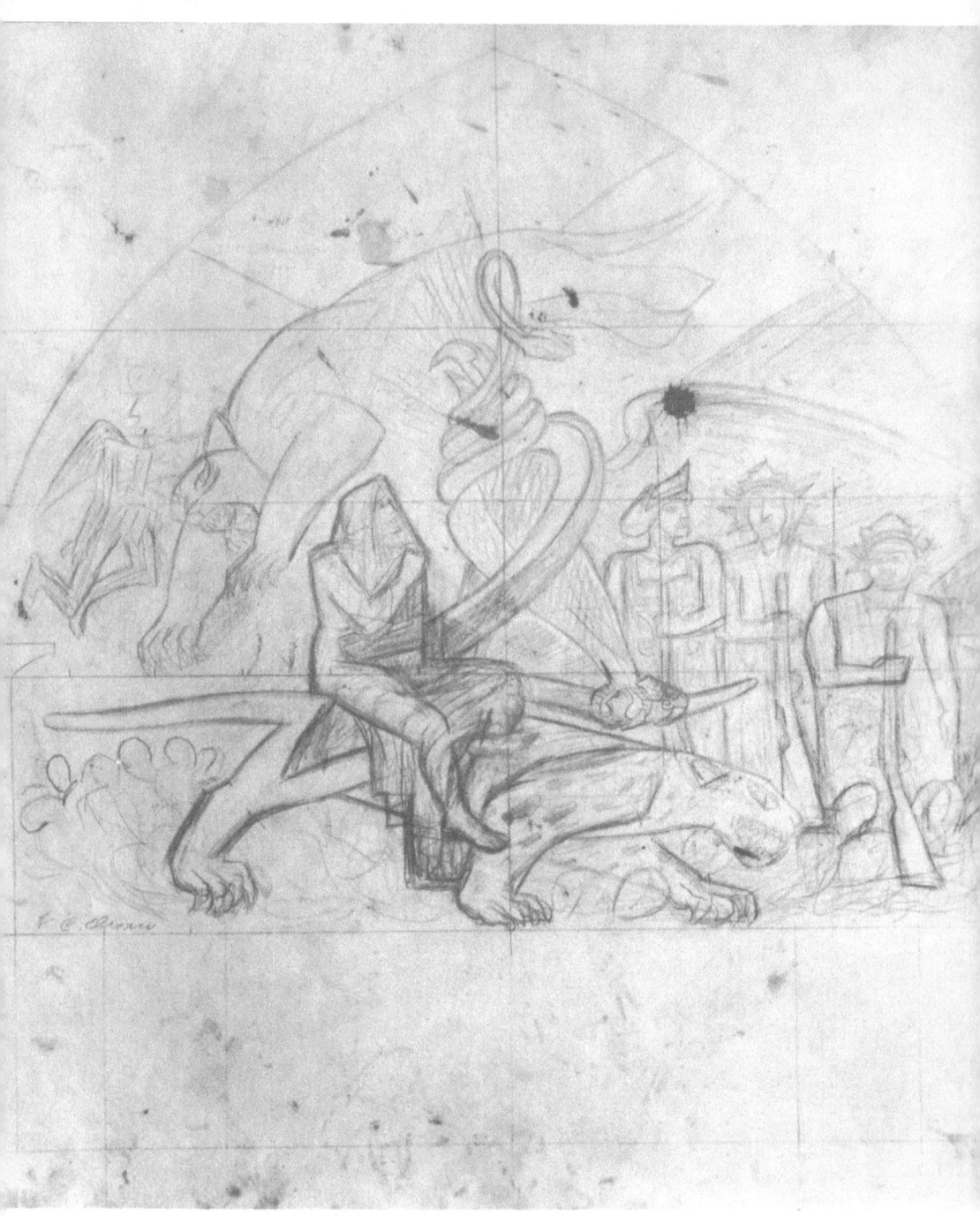

Allegory of Mexican Nationality. 1940.

Then they could be framed. I handled the brush and Galván made the frames. We could do the whole job in less than an hour and live on the proceeds for a week.

Galván would be off with his friends, and I along the coast, in the fantastic forests of trees that were already there thousands of years before the Christian Era and stand from three to six hundred feet high (according to the Chamber of Commerce); or I would visit the University of California, or the Bohemian quarters of San Francisco, with their cabarets, their dance halls, their Italian restaurants, and their saloons in the style of the Forty-niners, decorated with photographs of the most celebrated Mexican bandits of the time, that is, the dispossessed, who had been driven from their lands. Through this district, and through the studios of sculptors and painters there, passed the joyous, noisy, money-laden crowd which filled this world. I saw Chinatown, with its silks, its tinsel, its mystery. I encountered handsome and stately Negresses in search of "admirers," and robust blondes on the same quest. Revelry and madness were everywhere, and everywhere the Kaiser, with horns to match his mustache, was being thrust into the flames "to Make the World Safe for Democracy."

I admired the tattooing parlors, in which sailors are tattooed red, blue, and green, from head to foot, the favorite figures being an immense American flag and an eagle on the back, a portrait of a sweetheart on the chest, and lesser, merely decorative, designs on the belly, the legs, and the arms. The sailor has a great variety of patterns to choose from.

65

There was a restaurant called "Coppa," decorated by the many painters in San Francisco. Uprooted artists could dine there a few times in exchange for pictures drawn on the walls. Happily I was not reduced to painting anything for the Coppa. The time for murals had not yet arrived.

Art in San Francisco was one hundred percent academic. Even New York was as yet untouched by the Modern Art of the Paris School, with which as yet only a select minority was acquainted.

Tired of San Francisco, I determined to move on to New York. At the very moment when I was on my way to take the train and cross the continent, Woodrow Wilson was arriving on his tour of the country in support of the League of Nations. He stood in his automobile, smiling, his hat in his hand. The crowd was portentously silent, in sign of disagreement and protest. It was clear that the League was an intolerable farce.

At Niagara Falls, on my way, I crossed over to the Canadian side to admire the most beautiful of the cataracts. I had been there a couple of hours when a policeman detected something suspicious in my countenance and asked for my passport. On seeing that I was a Mexican he literally gave a jump and expelled me on the spot, himself conducting me back to the American side. The Prince of Wales was then visiting the neighborhood, and might be the object of an attempt upon his life. That same day newspapers, in enormous red headlines, had come out with a yellow journalist's account of how the Villistas had assaulted a train in Sonora and violated all the women passengers. "Mexican" and "bandit" were synonyms.

Chapter 7 Shocks and Conflicts. Mass Meetings. The Bearded Lady. Costumed Fleas. The Sermon on the Mount Falsified. The Donkey Paints a Picture.

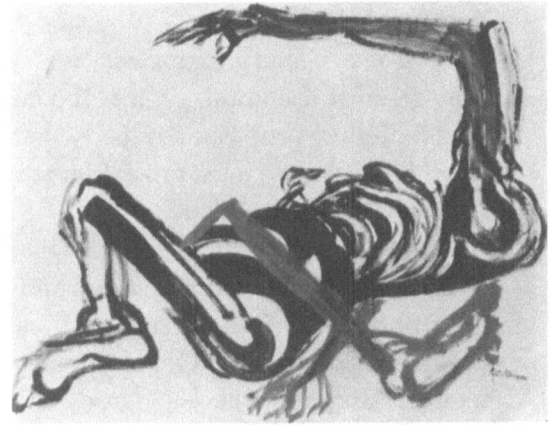

Corpse. 1943.

1n New York I encountered Siqueiros on the point of embarking for Europe with his wife, Graciela Amador.

We joined forces with Juan Olaguíbel and together saw the sights of the Empire City. By subway we went to Brooklyn, discussing the prodigies of mechanics in relation with the arts, and for the sake of a livelier evening we each took a different and challenging position. I have forgotten what my own stand was, but

71

I do, as I say, remember that I differed with them, and they with each other. Without conflict there would be no films, no bull fights, no journalism, no politics, no free struggle, nothing. Life would be most boring. As soon as anyone says "yes" it is necessary to answer "no." Everything should be done against the grain, against the current, and if some insensate fellow proposes a remedy that would do away with the difficulties, we must crush him at whatever cost, for civilization itself is at stake.

When Siqueiros had embarked and Olaguíbel gone off to do a portrait of Enrico Caruso, I set out to explore New York, and I discovered two of the nicest and most diverting scenes: Harlem, where Negroes and Spanish Americans live, and Coney Island. The latter is gigantic, a beach that will hold a million people on an outing. Those who speak of multitudes and mass meetings without having seen Coney Island on a summer afternoon have no notion of what they are talking about. The space at the disposal of each person is little more than five square feet, on the sand and in the water alike. Not that there isn't more beach and more water; but the holiday crowds like to be at peaceful close quarters together, everyone with his wife, his children, his friends, and his dogs. They arrive very early in the morning, they install themselves on the sand, they stretch out in the sun, and there they stay until well along in the night. It is particularly then, at night, that stupendous, marvelous things happen, for all Coney Island is brilliant with colored lights and the flare of fireworks.

72

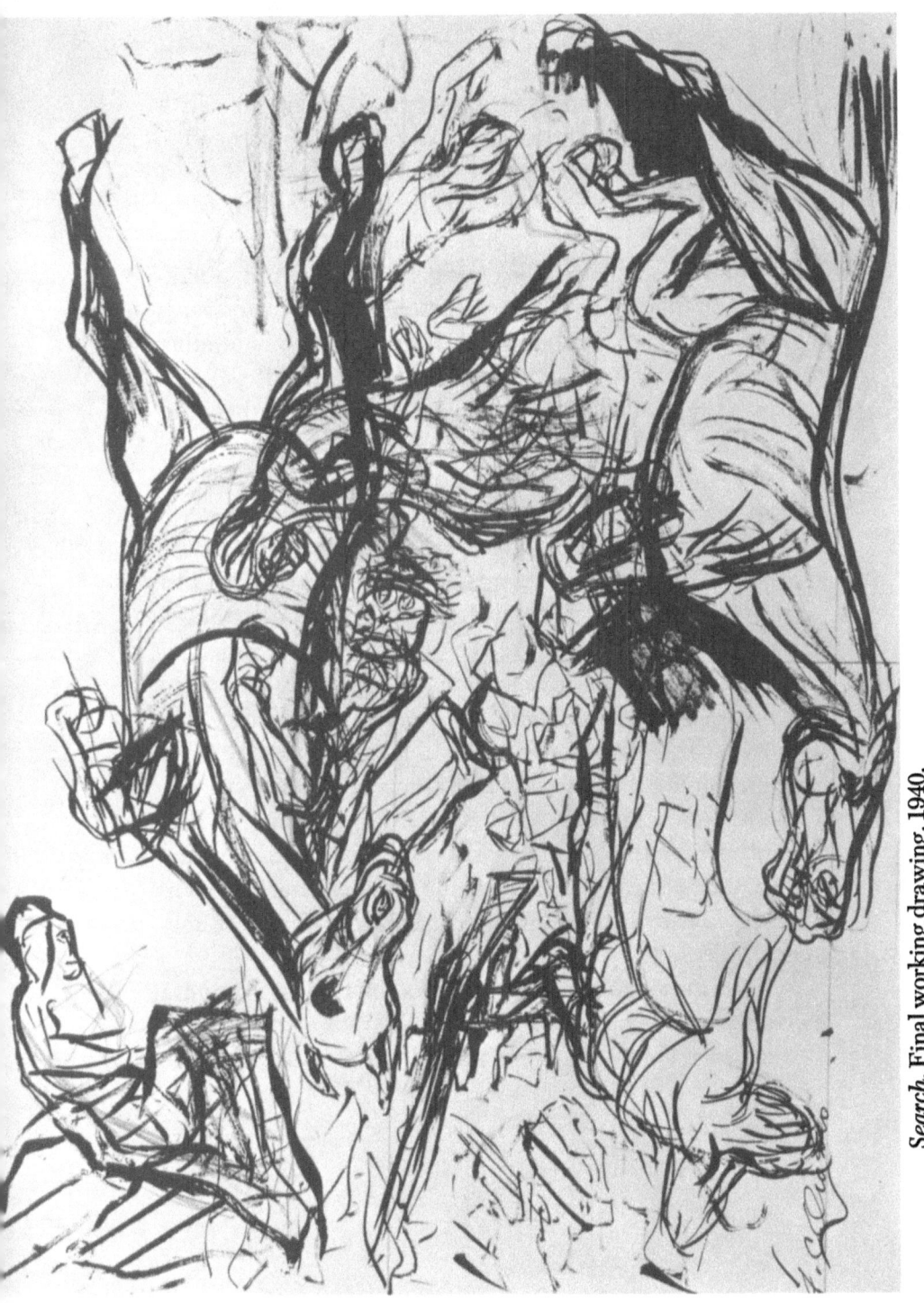

Search. Final working drawing, 1940.

Along the beach the great, the typical, American Fair is laid out, with endless attractions which there is no need to describe, since everyone, young and old, has heard of them. On the other hand, what does need to be described is the bearded lady, the fattest woman in the world, the ape man, the two-headed man, the midgets, the half-man-half-woman, and various other monstrosities. I afterwards learned that there is a bureau to supply whatever number of fattest women in the world are needed for all the side shows in the United States, or whatever bearded ladies. The midgets are small fry, and can be rented by the dozen. There is even an illustrated catalogue for the information of impresarios. We should find nothing particularly strange in this, for the Museum of Modern Art in New York in the same way rents out works of art for exhibitions. Cubist paintings by the lot, Surrealist, Dadaist, Mexican things, or particular combinations of Picasso-Braque, Picasso-Rouault, Picasso-Matisse, Picasso-Chirico, on order and at so much a week, to any club, university, or cocktail party that may want to spice things up with Modern Art.

Even the incubators for children are something to see. These are nothing like poultry hatcheries, but are a special apparatus to maintain an artificial climate for prematurely born or rachitic infants. Inside, the little ones are as comfortable as can be, and laugh and laugh in their confinement.

Next to these are the tattoo parlors for sailors, like those in San Francisco, but more varied.

Here great three-masters in full sail are tattooed onto the

ample chest of the sailor and down below the navel a siren will come to rest on an anchor. On one arm there will be a Hawaiian girl in a hula skirt, and when the arm moves she will dance the hula-hula with undulating hips, and on the other arm, or the legs, there will be pictures of the "babes," or girl friends, who have had their turn at making the sailor happy in each of the ports in which he has come ashore. Other sailors prefer a large portrait of Washington or Lincoln with the corresponding banner and eagle.

Farther along one comes upon the costumed fleas of the Flea Circus. The "artists" perform very seriously, doing quite varied turns. They swing, they balance on the seesaw, they do acrobatics, and they perform on the trapeze and the slack wire. Hitched in pairs they pull tiny paper carriages in which the fattest and most aristocratic of lady fleas loll back, dressed like princesses and queens. On each side of the carriage march pages, grooms, and lackeys, in hats, and behind them follows a long train of nobles and dignitaries of the court. It is clear that there are social classes even among fleas, and that these can be the source of civil war, since one of these days they will realize that they have red blood in their veins (the red blood they have sucked) and they will decapitate the fat fleas in the carriages.

A hundred and fifty thousand divisions of fleas, supported by forty-ton bedbug tanks, will close in a colossal pincers movement against the positions occupied by an enemy already softened up by waves of mosquito planes. Death and devastation. Hand-to-hand encounters. Bayonet charges.

Heaps of dead bodies. Planes and tanks will crash with horrid uproar and blood will run in torrents as the pincers close and the spectators at the Flea Circus scratch frantically.

In 1922 mural painting began in Mexico. But before speaking of it, we should examine the ideas that prevailed at the time. First we should mention Infantilism.

The primitive Impressionistic schools had undergone a radical transformation. They no longer simply tried to imitate the French Impressionists, to paint sunlight in the field and the sun itself, the air and the hour, forgetting objects in the effort to capture the wavering play of light on water. The "democratic" idea had emerged, a sort of artistic Christianity and the beginning of Nationalism. Students themselves were different. Instead of the student of art all sorts of people appeared, from schoolboys and truants to clerks, young ladies, workers, and peasants, the young as well as the old. They quite lacked previous training. Without more ado they were handed colors, canvas, and pencils and told to paint as they pleased whatever they had before them: landscapes, fruits, figures, or objects. The result was simply marvelous—stupendous—works of genius. There were no adjectives sufficiently eloquent to describe what they did. History, previous knowledge of geometry, perspective, anatomy, the theory of color were nothing but academicism, an obstacle in the way of freely expressing an undefined national genius. The professor had nothing to teach the students; on the contrary it was they who would teach him. Candor and innocence in children and simple folk were

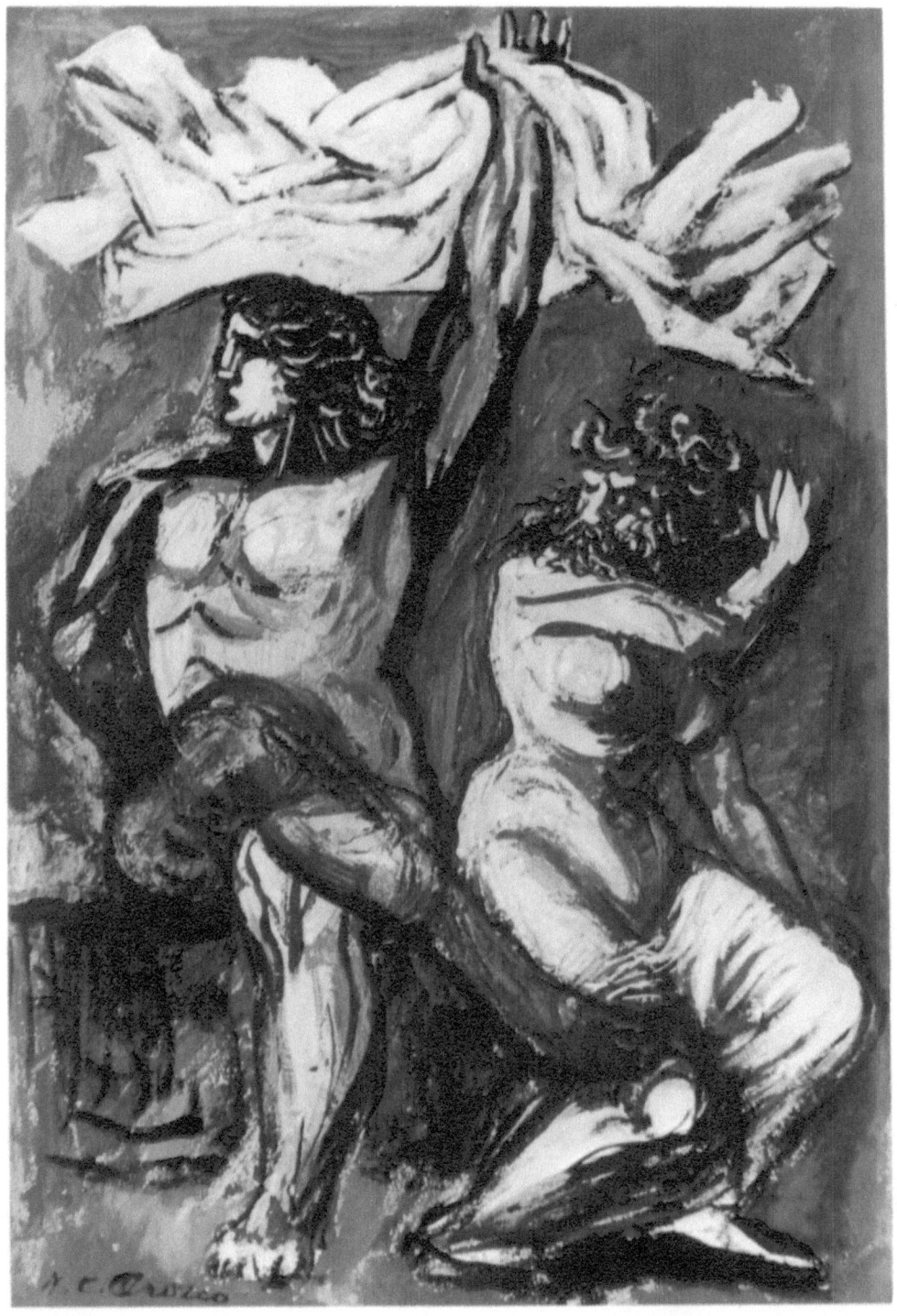

sacred qualities, not to be blighted with technical animad-versions, and the "student" was to hear only a litany of praise, and exclamations of wonder like the "Olés" that greet Armillita's cape work. The merit of a work was all the greater if the boy was illiterate, since his soul was still vir-ginal, immaculate, free of all contamination and prejudice. Let him reason ever so little and his work would suffer for it, it would no longer be innocent and spontaneous. Blessed are the ignorant and the imbecile, for theirs is the supreme glory of art! Blessed are the idiots and the cretins, for mas-terpieces of painting shall issue from their hands!

All that remained was to perform the experiment of the donkey painter. This was quite an ordinary donkey which was put into a position to paint. How? Very simply. Within range of its tail a palette was set up, provided with brilliant colors, and beside it a blank canvas. When the burro swished its tail, the colors hit the canvas, which was thor-oughly besmeared. The picture was carried to Paris, to a Salon of Modern Painting, where it was shown anony-mously, and the critics rapturously praised the audacity of the technique, the brilliance of the colors, and the mastery of execution; they considered it from philosophical and the-ological points of view; they quoted Plato and announced the dawn of a revolution in art.

Pictures from the open-air school actually were carried to Paris, I forget in what year. The great men of art and criti-cism who were invited to the showing were overwhelmed and proclaimed that the Mexican prodigy was the wonder of the ages.

It would have been interesting if the National Conservatory of Music, having for the same reasons suppressed all musical theory, training, and technique, had gone out onto the street in search of any prospects whatsoever, deaf men or suckling babes, taco venders, lottery-ticket sellers, or bus drivers, and sitting them down at the piano or handing them a violin had expected them without more ado to make music like Beethoven's.

Chapter 8   The Table Is Set. First

Efforts. The Painters, Their Critical Powers.

Jean Charlot. European Painting. Artists

Today.

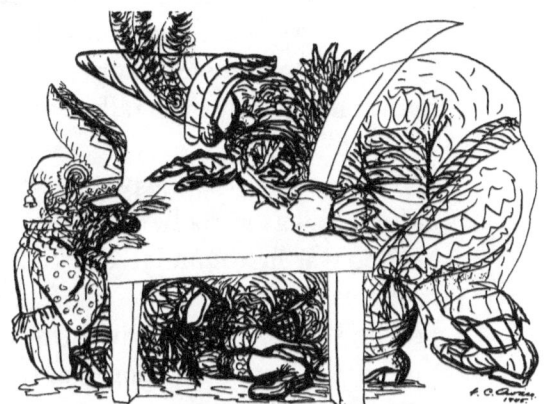

Intimidation of Smaller Buffoon. 1945.

By 1922 the table was set for mural painting. The very idea of doing murals, along with other ideas which were to make up the new artistic epoch, and animate it, was already there and had developed throughout the twenty years from 1900 to 1920. Naturally, such ideas had their origin in past centuries but they acquired their definitive shape in these two decades. We all of us know, only too well, that no historical event occurs in isolation and without a cause.

We can summarize Mexican thought about art in the year 1920.

1. It had come to be believed that anyone could paint and that the greater the ignorance and stupidity of the painter, the greater the value of his work.

2. Many people held that pre-Cortesian Art was our true tradition and they even talked of a "renaissance of indigenous art."

3. Excitement over the plastic work of the contemporary indigenes was at its height. This was the moment when Mexico was first inundated with articles of woven straw, stewpots, huaraches, dancing figures from Chalma, serapes, and rebozos, and when the wholesale export of all this began. It was the apogee of the tourist trade in Cuernavaca and Taxco.

4. There was popular art in all its forms, in painting, in sculpture, in the theatre, in music, and in literature.

5. Extreme nationalism put in an appearance. Mexican artists considered themselves the equals or the superiors of foreigners. Their themes had necessarily to be Mexican.

6. The cult of the Worker was more sharply defined: "Art at the service of the Worker." It was believed that art must be essentially an offensive weapon in the Conflict of the Classes.

7. Dr. Atl's attitude of direct and active intervention in militant politics had shaped a school.

8. Artists were passionately preoccupied with sociology and history.

82

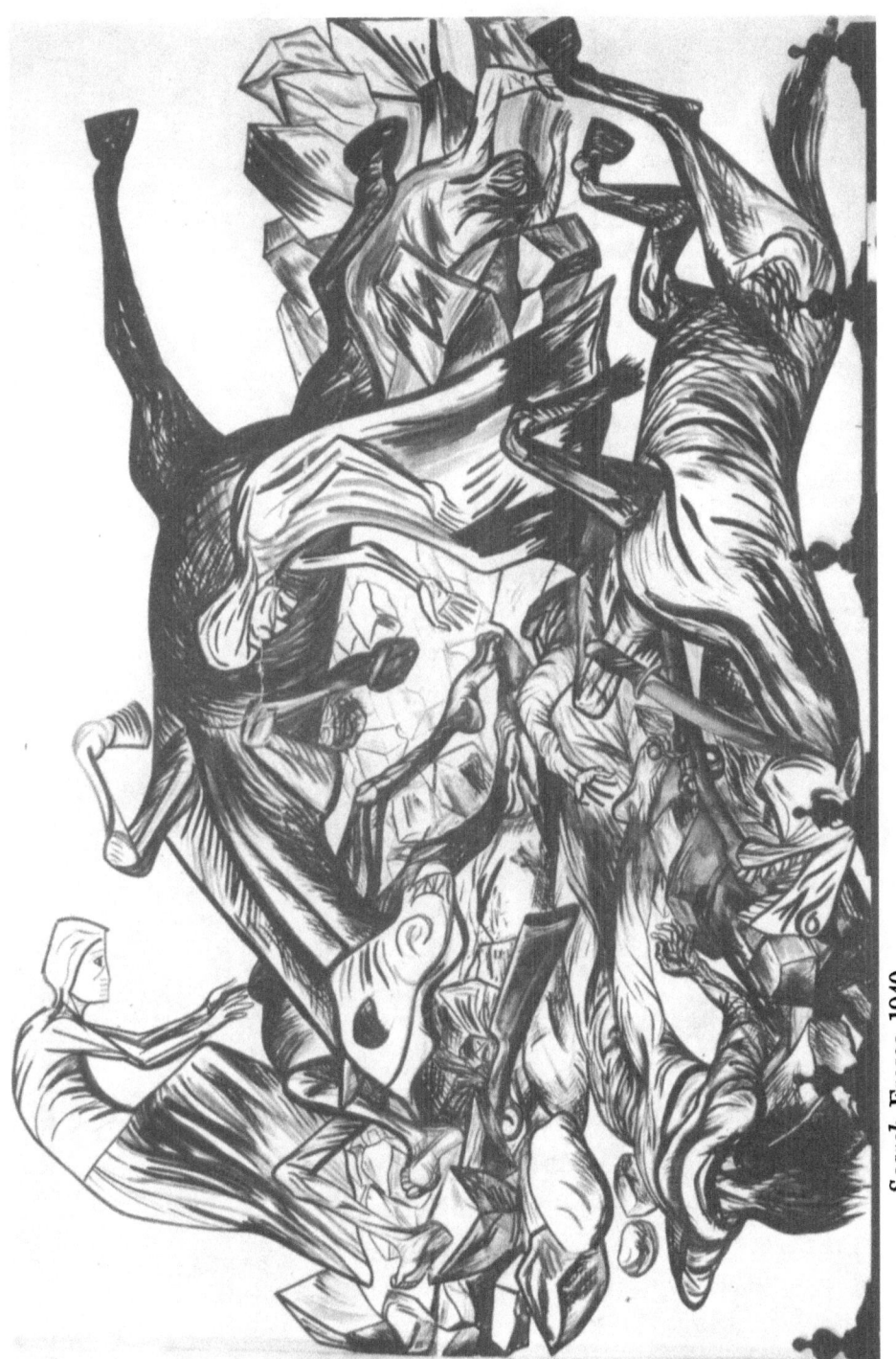

Search. Fresco. 1940.

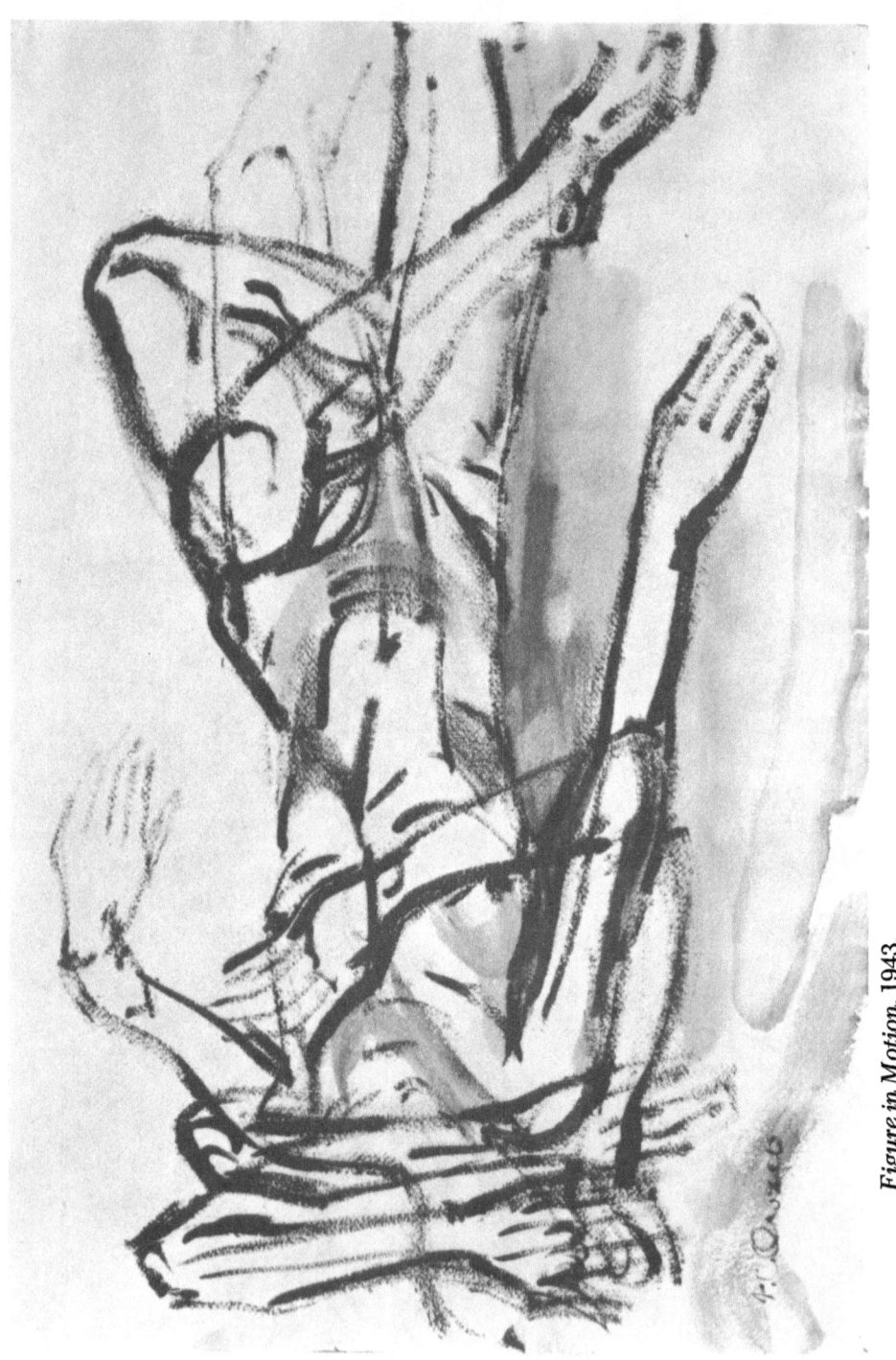

Figure in Motion. 1943.

It is interesting to point out that music had come to take a similar position at the time. In 1913 Manuel M. Ponce, before anyone else, had realized the value and significance of popular music, and at a concert of songs like "Estrellita," which he gave in Wagner Hall, he was hissed and censured for treating things seriously which had been held of no account.

These ideas were transformed and embodied in mural painting, but not all at once, for it was necessary, first, to find a technique which none of the painters yet commanded. Consequently, there was a time of preparation, during which much trial and error went on and the works produced were purely decorative, with only timid allusions to history, philosophy, and various other themes. Once the artists were in possession of the new technique, they used it extensively to express themselves, and, being a tight-knit group, picked up discoveries from one another.

Later, some of them came to cherish the theme of the painting with such passion that they completely abandoned the field of art and gave themselves over to activities no longer bearing any relation to their profession.

What distinguishes the mural painters from any other similar group is their critical gift. Thanks to the early training that most of them had had, they were in a position to see the actual problem clearly enough and to know which road to follow. They were fully aware of the historical moment in which it was given them to work, and of the relations of their art to the world and the society around them. By a

85

happy accident a group of experienced artists and revolutionary statesmen who understood the role of the artist joined forces in one and the same field of action. First among the statesmen was José Vasconcelos.

In 1922 the radically new Secretariat of Public Education was organized; the building for this was on the point of completion, and new schools, stadiums, and libraries were going up all around. From the Publishing Department, another of Vasconcelos' creations, editions of the classics in great numbers appeared and sold at less than cost for the benefit of the public. Artists and intellectuals were summoned to collaborate, and painters had such an opportunity as they had not known in centuries. I do not remember how or why Rivera returned from Europe. But Siqueiros was called home from Rome and the two rejoined the artists who had remained in Mexico. Jean Charlot joined them too, a French painter and army officer who had recently arrived in Mexico at the age of twenty-three.

Painters who had been in Europe brought their foreign experience and in particular their acquaintance with the Parisian School, preparation which was both useful and necessary in relating Mexican art to that of Europe. In this respect Jean Charlot was of special help, since he was a European painter exclusively—French and extremely young. That is to say, he represented European sensibility in its most modern and unprejudiced form. In general, with brilliant exceptions, the professors of aesthetics who visit us are fossils, arrested in their development at some time back in the eighteenth or nineteenth century, convinced that art can exist only in Paris as the heir to Rome, applying in some tortured sense the phrase about Paris being "the mind of the world," and viewing everything through the eyeglass of their antiquated library of erudition.

Charlot often tempered our youthful violence with his culture and equanimity, and illumined our problems with his lucid vision. He used to go along with us to the Museum of Archeology, where the great Aztec sculptures are on view. They impressed him profoundly and we would talk for hours of that tremendous art, which comes down to us and outstrips us, reaching out into the future. Pre-Cortesian Art influenced him to such an extent that his painting is still saturated with it.

The technical and aesthetic means at the disposal of the muralists in 1922 may be divided into two groups. First, there were those that came from Italy, and second, those that came from Paris. Not a one of the painters of the time, or later, has tried to paint in the Mayan, the Toltecan, the Chinese, or the Polynesian manner. Their painting comes from the Mediterranean or it comes with the manners and modes of the Paris that existed up until the recent totalitarian war and now seems gone forever. Of course the schools were not all necessarily French. Paris was a sort of Bourse of artistic values for all Europe and above all a market. It was the dealers who largely contributed to the development and expansion of the so-called Parisian School, which embraced contributions from around the world, even from

Mexico—witness the Douanier Rousseau, who had been a soldier in Bazaine's army when it invaded Mexico.

Mural painting began under good auspices. Even the errors it committed were useful. It broke with the routine into which painting had fallen. It disposed of many prejudices and served to reveal social problems from a new point of view. It liquidated a whole epoch of brutalizing Bohemianism, of frauds who lived the life of a drone in their ivory towers—their fetid dens—where, drunkenly strumming on their guitars, they kept up a pretense of absurd idealism, beggars in a society that was already rotten and close to extinction.

The painters and sculptors of the coming time would be men of action, strong, sound, well trained; ready like a good laborer to work eight or ten hours a day. They found their way into shops, universities, barracks, and schools, eager to learn and understand everything, and as soon as possible to do their part in creating a new world. They wore overalls and mounted the scaffoldings.

Chapter 9

The Syndicate of Painters and Sculptors. The Manifesto. Socialization of Art. Bourgeois Art and Proletarian Art. Rectifications.

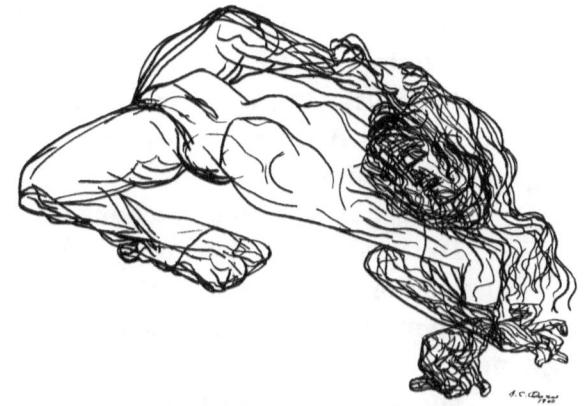

The Truth Twisted, Deformed, Altered, Mutilated, Daubed.

One of the truly singular manifestations of the critical gifts of these artists was the constitution of the Syndicate of Painters and Sculptors, which found condensed expression in an extraordinarily important manifesto and has gone on exerting an influence still to be felt after two decades, at a time when the younger painters have vainly struggled against it.

The Syndicate proper was of no consequence, not being a group of workers forced to struggle against an employer, but the name served as a banner for ideas in gestation, ideas based upon contemporary socialistic theories with which Siqueiros, Rivera, and Xavier Guerrero were most conversant.

Siqueiros formulated, and we accepted and signed, a "manifesto" directed at such soldiers, workers, farmers, and intellectuals as were out from under subservience to the bourgeoisie. In brief it expressed the following purposes:

"To socialize art.

"To destroy bourgeois individualism.

"To repudiate easel painting and any other art that emanated from ultra-intellectual and aristocratic circles.

"To produce only monumental works for the public domain.

"The moment being historical, in transition from a decrepit order to a new one, to realize a rich art for the people instead of an expression of individual pleasure.

"To create beauty which should suggest struggle and serve to arouse it."

Afterwards these purposes were modified in expression but in no fundamental sense.

Siqueiros came into contact with radical ideas in Europe. As military attaché to the Mexican Diplomatic Corps in Barcelona he pronounced a subversive discourse in the obsequies of a Mexican Anarchist, Del Toro, who had been slain by the police. He was expelled from the country and went to live in Argenteuil, France, where he attended Communist meetings of workers. There he absorbed the ideas that went into the Manifesto, and returning to Mexico in 1921, recalled by Vasconcelos, he brought the complete plan of a revolutionary art, the one he offered us.

Naturally, the socialization of art was a project for the distant future, since it implied a radical change in the structure of society. Besides, it was necessary to give a definite meaning to the word *socialize* as it applied to art, inasmuch as there had been many and diverse interpretations.

The repudiation of easel painting did not occur at all. Clearly it was unreasonable, for easel painting was in no way opposed to mural painting; it was merely different, and quite as useful as the other for popular purposes. So it was called "movable" painting, but it remained the same thing. Not only paintings, however, but small engravings too were considered necessary—to provide each worker's home with a work of art. It appeared further that some of the painters had no talent for doing murals, their gifts lying rather in the field of these smaller works.

To condemn easel painting as aristocratic was to condemn a great part of the art of all ages. The Rembrandts, the Titians, and the El Grecos would have to be destroyed.

By this road we reached the so-called "proletarian art," legitimate offspring of the Syndicate. Proletarian art consisted in pictures of workers on the job, and it was supposedly intended for them. But this turned out to be an error, since a worker who has spent eight hours in the shop takes no pleasure in coming home to a picture of workers on the job. He wants something different, which has nothing to do with work but serves the purposes of repose. On the other hand the comical thing about it all was that the bourgeois bought proletarian art at fancy prices, though it was supposed to be directed at them, and the proletarians would gladly have bought bourgeois art if they had had the money and, for want of it, found an agreeable substitute in calendar chromos: aristocratic maidens indolently reclining on bearskin rugs, or a most elegant-looking gentleman kissing a marquise by the light of the moon on a castle terrace. The halls in bourgeois homes are full of proletarian furniture and objects, like sleeping mats, cane-bottomed chairs, clay pots and tin candlesticks; whereas a worker, as soon as he has money enough to furnish his house, buys a pullman sofa in heavy velvet, a breakfast set, or a set of those extra rare pieces of furniture built of nickel-plated iron tubings, thick crystals, and beveled mirrors.

Shoe shops in León and Guadalajara produce enormous quantities of huaraches for the bourgeois of the United States, while our serving girls are dying to have high-heeled shoes and a pair of silk stockings.

Madero Avenue and Juárez Avenue are full of shops which sell proletarian goods. To buy silks you have to go to Lagunilla.

The truth is that good taste is not always innate or the exclusive patrimony of a given race or class. Only education can create or refine it.

At the moment of fervent Indigenism we identified the Indian with the proletarian, without taking into account

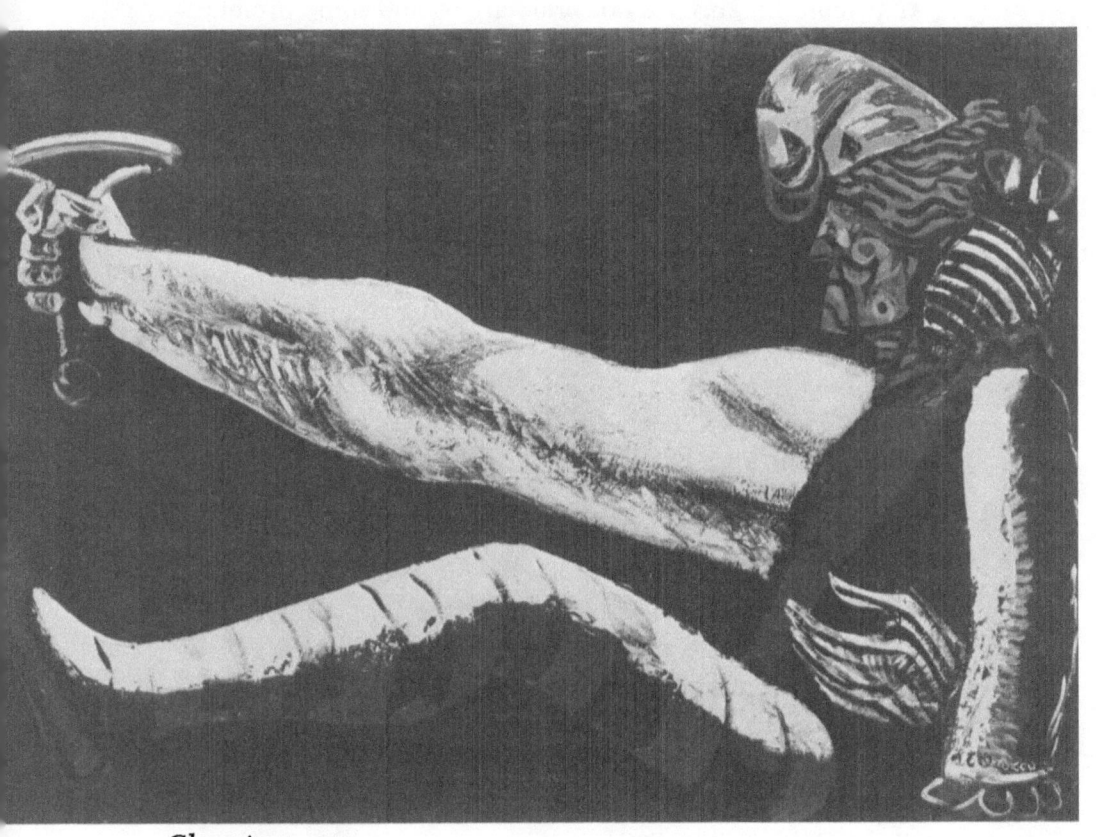

Clowning.

that some Indians are not proletarians and some proletarians are not Indians, and the results were the Indo-proletarian pictures, which were likewise children of the Syndicate. All these pictures wound up in the United States in the hands of the white race. Neither the Indians down here nor those up there had any notion of pictures thus exalting them. In the United States it came to be believed that Mexican painters were tremendously popular among the indigenous masses, as Zapata might be, though Zapata himself may be utterly unknown to the indigenes of Durango or Quintana Roo.

The Manifesto likewise promised combat painting, to incite the oppressed to a struggle for liberation. This point remains too obscure for us to ascertain precisely what it means. When is a painting or a piece of sculpture really calculated to arouse mental processes that will turn into revolutionary action in the viewer? When is it really subversive? It is true that the Catholic Church has used the arts in general and the plastic arts in particular to quicken faith and devotion. The believer always responds to a Crucifixion or a Dolorosa; but it is also true that in mosques and Protestant churches, where there are no images, the same quickening of faith is to be observed.

Instances of the arts exerting a decisive revolutionary influence upon the spectator must be conditioned by some factors as yet unknown and others of a purely fortuitous nature. Hearing the "International" or the national anthem sung by twenty thousand people in the plaza, while the flags are rippling in the sunshine and the bells are sounding and

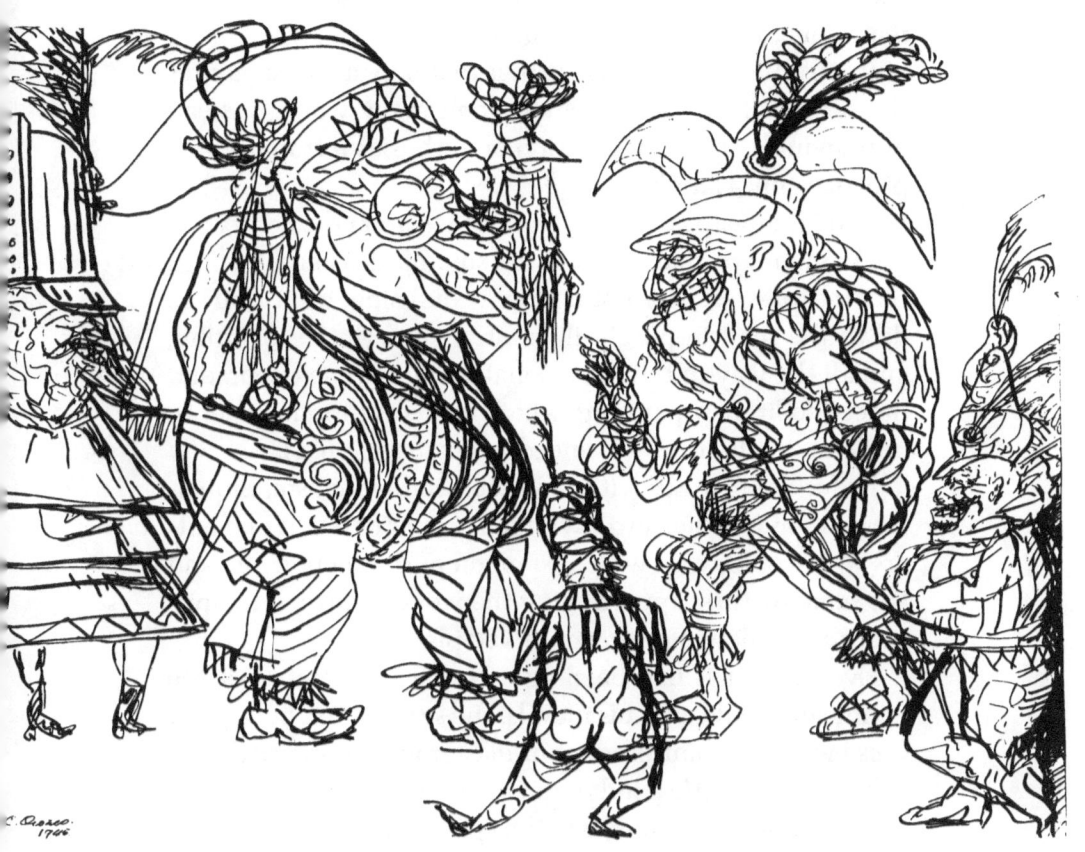

Meeting of Buffoons (grotesque).

the sirens are deafening us, is not the same thing as hearing it all alone, at home, on the phonograph.

It must be remembered further that only a line separates the sublime from the ridiculous, and many works, instead of drawing a cry of indignation or enthusiasm from us may provoke only a laugh.

The Manifesto laid great importance upon the content of the work of art, that is, upon the sum of ideas and feelings that it expresses. This notion too is confusing, for it leads us down the road to purely illustrative, descriptive painting, and all the way to the impersonal photographic document, indeed to literary painting, which neglects form in order to declaim or tell stories—to anecdotal painting, that is.

As for doing away with bourgeois individualism, Siqueiros and Xavier Guerrero envisaged groups or teams of painters who would work with a common purpose upon one and the same picture, apportioning the work according to aptitudes and following a preconceived plan.

Even earlier it had been agreed that no member of the Syndicate would sign his murals, the supposition being that these were the joint product of master and apprentices and subject to the critical judgment of all the painters. This idea failed, for no one would keep the agreement.

Later on, teams really did function, but insufficiently to show with any certainty what results they might have. It is possible that in given cases collective work may be necessary in a single painting or piece of sculpture. The result would be quite different from that achieved by a single artist. But the latter cannot efface himself from the work as the Manifesto seems to hope.

Another interpretation of the idea is that all the while he is creating, the artist should have the collectivity in mind, or the society of which he forms a part, and not the purpose of affording pleasure to an individual only or a small number of individuals. But even here is confusion. Art interests everybody but unfortunately non-art interests everybody equally as much, if not more. The world is bursting with vulgarities known and enjoyed by millions of people in every land. The worst movies last longest.

The problem can be put another way: is the artist going to impose his work upon the collectivity by "force or reason," as the Chileans say, or is the collectivity going to impose its tastes and preferences upon the artist? We must first know which collectivity is in question, which social class, which race, what age, what level of education. It would be interesting, again, to know whether the given collectivity as such will make the decision directly or whether it will do so through representatives, for we then must likewise know who the representatives are, and how they can faithfully interpret the tastes of their constituents. Above all, we need to know whether the collectivity really has a taste. But of course it has: it mostly likes sugar, honey, and candy. Diabetic art. The greater the amount of sugar, the greater the—commercial—success.

Chapter 10   The History
of Mexico. Indians, Spaniards, and
Mestizos. How the Conquest Should
Have Gone.

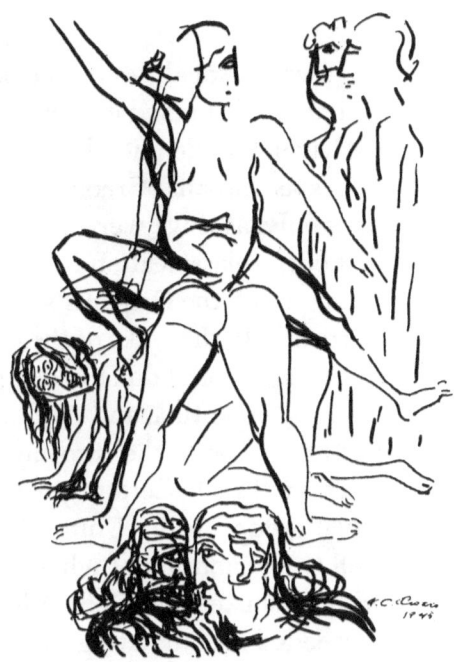

Composition of Seven Figures.

Τhe theme that has occupied the muralists most is the history of Mexico. Some of them have followed one faction or another of historians, others have taken their own independent line, but each of them has become a source of expert opinion and penetrating and forceful comment. This is really most remarkable. The discrepancies, from painting to painting, are a reflection of anarchy and confusion in historical studies themselves, a cause or an effect of

103

our own personality not yet being clear in mind, however well defined it may be in behavior. Like victims of amnesia we haven't found out who we are. We go on classifying ourselves as Indians, Creoles, and mestizos, following blood lines only, as if we were discussing race horses, and the effect of the classification is to divide us into implacable partisan groups, the Hispanists and the Indigenists, who war to the death. In the wake of these, other groups will be shaped by immigration. I don't know, perhaps there is a Pro-Italian Party in Argentina, and perhaps the Pro-Germans, the Pro-Portuguese and the Pro-Japanese are at one another's throats in Brazil. Certainly there is deep hatred between the racial groups in the United States and it would be just as well to say nothing of what we find in Europe. The whole world is shaken and bled with racial hatred. No religion has succeeded in eliminating it.

In Mexico history seems to have been written throughout from the racial point of view alone. Discussion apparently reduces to proclaiming or imposing the superiority of one or the other of the two races, and the worst of it is that this is no merely domestic argument, for foreign pens have intervened and go on intervening in the composition, with mischievous intent. The efforts of our historians might be a prize fight between an Indianist and a Hispanist, with a foreigner for referee.

Upon the theory that Mexico is necessarily indigenous, Spanish, or mixed of race, we can base only a false definition of personality. By Spanish we mean not a single race but

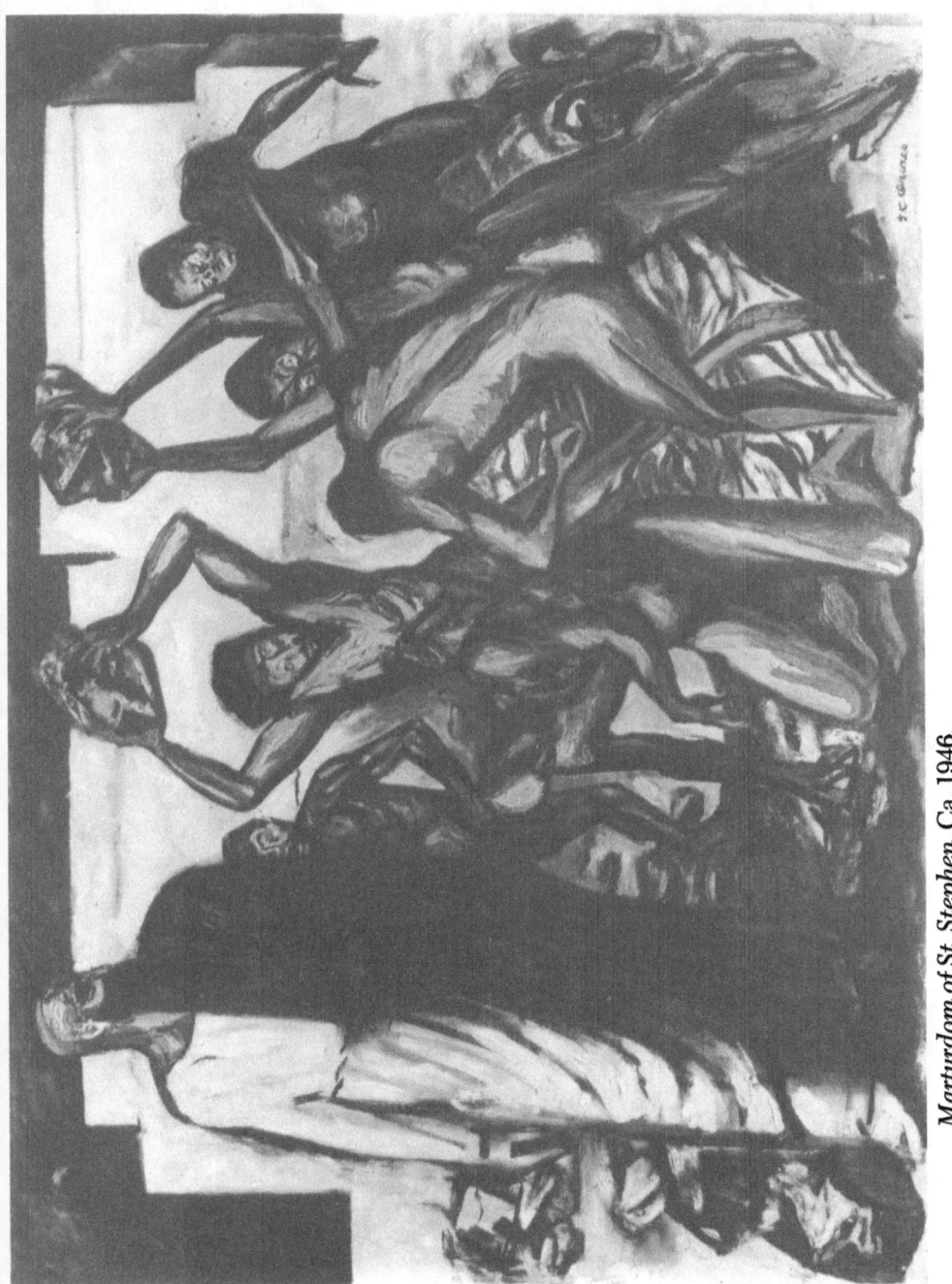

Martyrdom of St. Stephen. Ca. 1946.

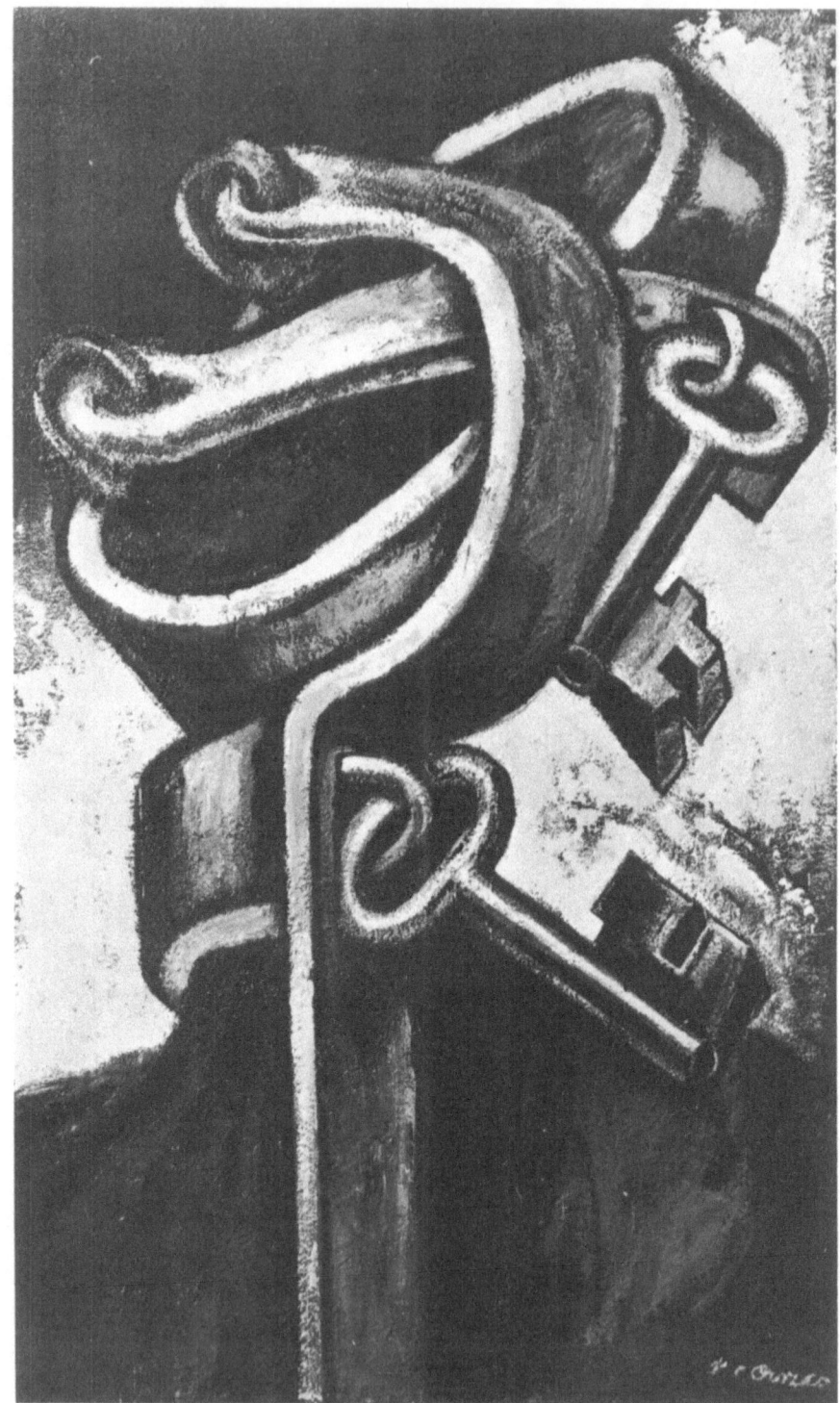

many and diverse races. Spain was the work of Iberians, Celts, Romans, Greeks, Phoenicians, Jews, Arabs, Goths, Berbers, and Gypsies, and each of these groups was in turn a mixed one. Of what race were the Spaniards and the Portuguese who have been coming to the Americas for the past four hundred years?

In modern times other races have been added to those from Spain and Portugal in Spanish America, or rather, all the races of the earth have been added in considerable numbers. Moreover, the indigenes themselves were apparently of no single racial stock, to judge by their diversity of types, customs, language, and native stages of culture.

The racial thesis, or theory, when applied to the exclusion of any other, works serious harm. Racial antagonism is exacerbated. It becomes as if Hernando Cortés and his soldiers had conquered Mexico only yesterday. At any given moment the Conquest looms more immediate than the forays of Pancho Villa. The attack upon Great Teocalli, the Noche Triste, and the destruction of Tenochtitlán did not take place early in the sixteenth century, but just last year. Discussion goes on with as much rancor as in the days of Antonio de Mendoza. Such antagonism is fatal, for all races are proud in the extreme. None of them will admit defeat or accept final submission. They will concede that they have lost a battle, but they await a day of revenge, which may be delayed but will come sooner or later, without fail, and then the victims of yesterday will be the victors of tomorrow. This, precisely this, is the leprosy of wars of independence, the leprosy that comes from abroad, the hatred of the Span-

107

Head of Slave.

iard. Bolívar promised violence, against the guilty and the innocent alike. His was a professional hatred, at the service of his own party. Later he realized that he had been plowing the waves.

To achieve unity, peace, and progress, it would be enough, perhaps, to dismiss the racial question for good and all. No more talk of Indians, Spaniards, and mestizos. Only theoretical studies of the Conquest, and these kept strictly within their corresponding bounds, that is, within discussion of the sixteenth century. The Indian considered not as an "Indian" but as a man, the equal of any other, just as the Andalusian or the Basque is. If we must have a Department of Indian Affairs, why not one of Creole Affairs or Mestizo Affairs? A Department of Indian Affairs sounds like a Department of Poor Devils, a Department of Unfortunate Minors, incapable of doing for themselves and standing in need of another race to think for them and graciously provide them with their wants, in token return for three centuries of colonial exploitation. Such a department is a magnificent sinecure, with the motto "Humor the poor devil even if he hasn't a leg to stand on"—advice we follow in dealing with madmen, though the Indian may have nothing of the madman in his make-up. A Department of the Vicious or the Sickly would be less humiliating. Indigenous races are nothing but an item more in the Hispanic total, with the categorical rights of any other group. If we forgot the divisive topic of races, there would be no more need to speak of the lioness and her cubs, or the mother and her sons. We should all of us be the lion, and all of us Mother Spain, from

108

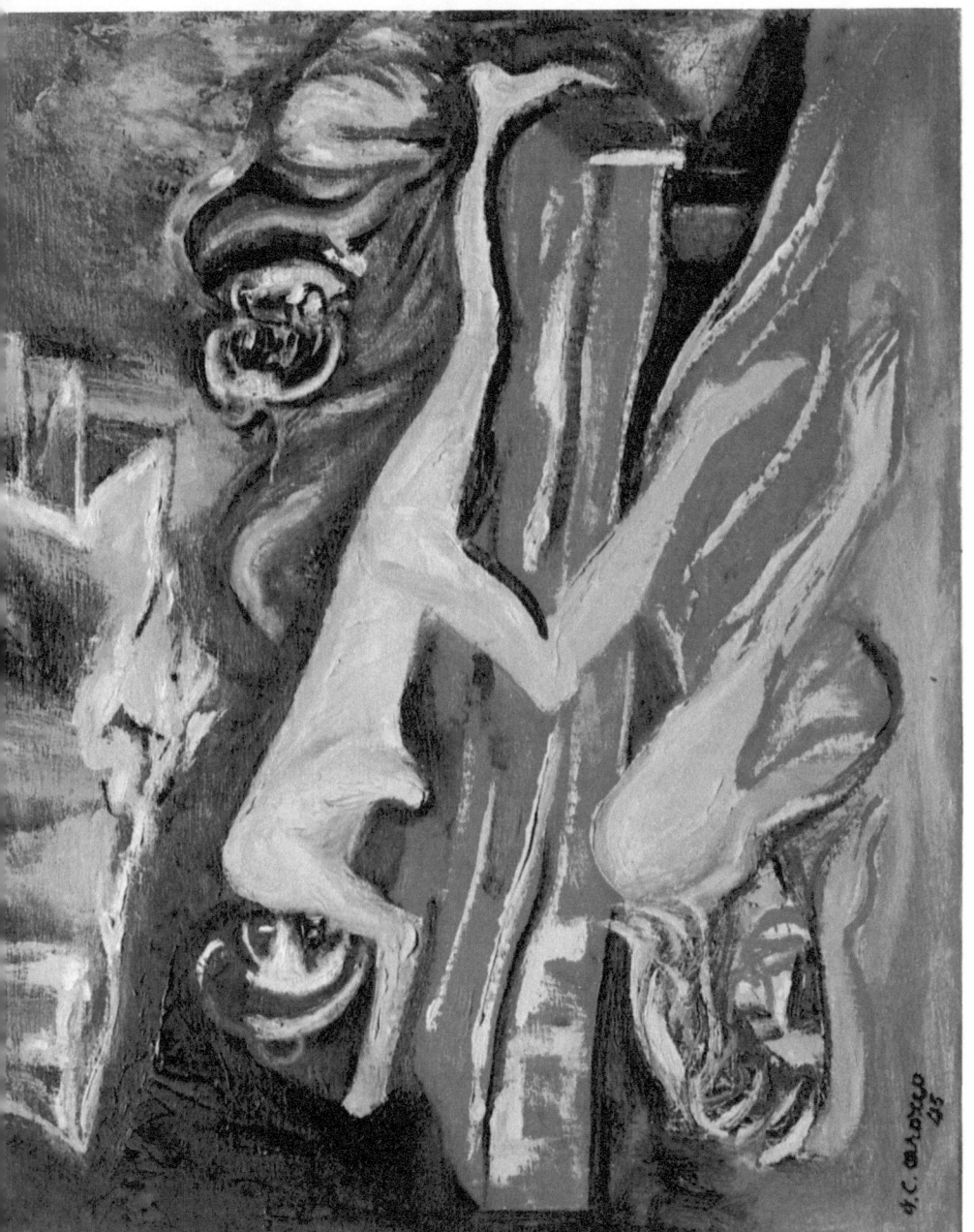

Asylum Scene.

Catalonia to Peru, from Chihuahua to Patagonia. The metropolis could be found, the world over, wherever a Spanish folk was living, thinking, loving.

But this attractive and sweeping view is marred by the Indigenists. According to them the Conquest ought not to have taken place as it did. Instead of sending cruel and ambitious captains to the New World, Spain should have sent a great delegation of ethnologists, anthropologists, archeologists, civil engineers, dentists, veterinarians, physicians, country school-teachers, agronomists, Red Cross nurses, philosophers, philologists, biologists, art critics, mural painters, and learned historians. On reaching Vera Cruz the caravels should have unloaded carriages, adorned with symbolical floral designs, with Cortés and his captains in one of them, carrying baskets of lilies and a great many other flowers and confetti and paper ribbon on the way to render homage to powerful Moctezuma and afterwards to set up bacteriological, urological, X-ray, and ultra-violet-ray laboratories, a Department of Public Works, universities, kindergartens, libraries, and banking houses. Instead of accepting the Aztec and Toltec maidens so frequently offered to them, the Spaniards should have brought along nice-looking girls from Galicia and Andalusia as gifts to Moctezuma and Cuauhtémoc. Alvarado, Ordaz, Sandoval, and other stout fellows should have been detailed to guard the ruins lest any least bit of the tremendous pre-Cortesian Art be lost. They should have learned the seven hundred and eighty-two distinct languages that were spoken here. They should have respected the indigenous religion and left Huitzilo-pochtli standing. There should have been a free distribution of grain, cattle, and agricultural machinery. Free housing could have been provided for the country folk, and common landholdings and cooperatives established. Roads and bridges might have been built. There were new industries and sports to inculcate, all in the best manner, gently and affectionately. Human sacrifice might have been encouraged further, and a great packing house built for human flesh, with a department to handle canning and refrigeration. Very tactfully it might have been suggested to Great Moctezuma that he should establish democracy for the lower orders, while preserving the privileges of the aristocracy and thus pleasing everyone.

In this way the three abhorrent centuries of the Colonial Period could have been side-stepped, and Great Teocalli would still be standing, though thoroughly disinfected to keep the blood of sacrifices from going bad, and to enable us to turn it into blood pudding—in a factory standing where, for want of it, the National Pawnshop inadequately serves.

How nice it would have been if the guests to appear at the monstrous banquet with which the newspaper *National Life* celebrated its silver anniversary had all come in breech-clout and feather headdress, armed with flint knives, and the uproar that drowned out the orators had been a bab-bling in the 1,320 indigenous tongues. Obviously *Excelsior* would have been written in Chichimeca.

Chapter 11 The Machete.

The United Group of the Working Class Movement. Asúnsolo and His Stonecutters. Vandalism. Fanfare. Pulque-Shop Painting.

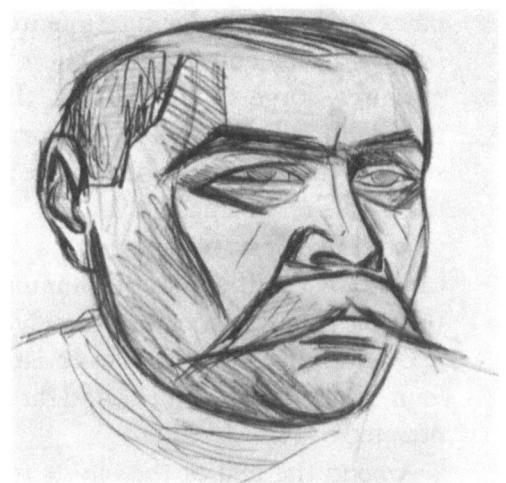

Head of a Mexican Peasant.

After launching their Manifesto, the Syndicate of Painters and Sculptors resolved to publish a weekly
paper to represent them. They put Siqueiros
in charge of it and called it *The Machete*. But
it would never have succeeded without the indispensable collaboration of Graciela Amador.
Siqueiros furnished the general political no-
tions, with the approval of the Syndicate, but
she edited most of the articles and composed

113

the magnificent ballads that came to be the essential stuff of the publication. The illustrations were furnished by the painters, in particular by Siqueiros himself, Xavier Guerrero, and Clemente Orozco. These were woodcuts or photogravures. Jorge Piñó Sandoval, then quite young, folded, bundled, and delivered the paper, and posted notices on street walls. He began his brilliant journalistic career with the ABC's of the trade.

After five or six numbers had appeared *The Machete* was turned over to the infant Communist Party, represented at the time by a small committee only.

Our original drawings were later bought by the Petroleum Workers of Tampico, and the money they brought was donated to *The Machete*.

Among the first of the efforts to interest intellectuals in workers' problems was the founding of a group called "The Joint Group of the Working-Class Movement." The founders were: Vicente Lombardo Toledano, Director of the Preparatory School; Henríquez Ureña; Toussaint; Caso; Rivera; the lawyer Enrique Delhumeau; the writer of these lines; and others whose names I have forgotten. The last two named on the list above were commissioned to organize local committees in Morelia and Guadalajara, with which object we set out. But the only responses to our call came from Bohemians of the sort that indifferently attend a wedding or a Communist or a Fascist meeting, or go to a circus or whatever turns up: the young ladies who recite romantic verses and village anarchists of the most inoffensive type.

114

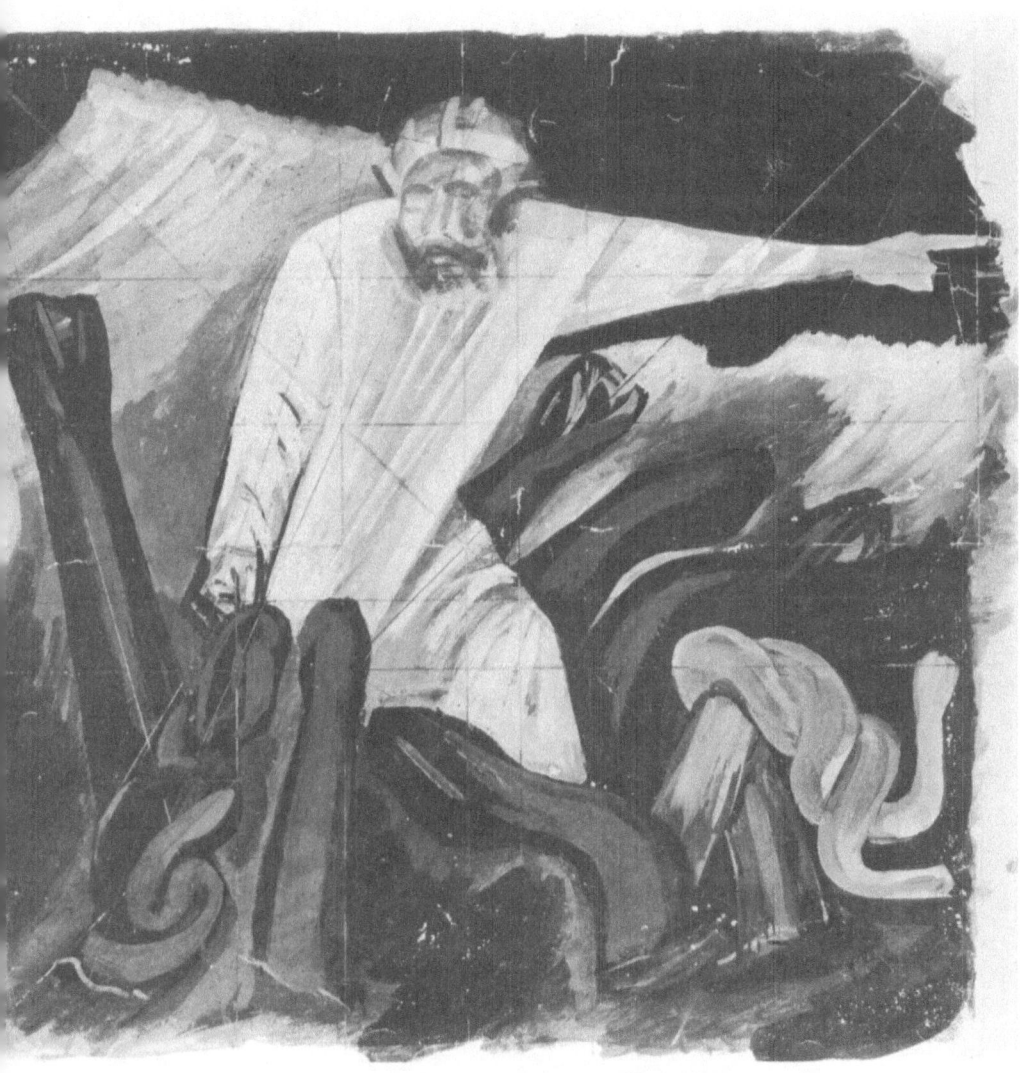

The Departure of Quetzalcoatl. Composition, right half.

Painting was all the while invading the walls. Heroic compositions, experiments, enthusiasm, envy, intrigues, apprenticeship.

Students in the Preparatory School did not take kindly to the painting. It is safe to say that none of them liked it, and they frequently protested to the Secretariat of Education, so that Ignacio Asúnsolo, learning how they were taking things, presented himself in the School one morning, at the head of sixty stonecutters he employed, and opening fire with his forty-five, emptied the three cartridge belts he was wearing, all the while that he and his brigade were shouting death to students who resist beauty. Asúnsolo was working on sculptures that were to decorate the façade and the patios of the Secretariat; at pistol point he had to defend himself against the carpers, our common enemy.

On another occasion ladies of the Red or the Green Cross, I don't quite remember which, needed the main patio of the School for a charity bazaar; but instead of politely asking me to suspend my work for a few days, they haughtily ordered me to withdraw, had my scaffoldings dismantled on the spot, and hung ornaments for the bazaar directly over the pictures in process. They were loud-voiced in their disapproval and their disgust. In particular the nude figure of a woman with a child displeased them; they believed that it was a Virgin. But I had had no intention of painting a virgin, I was painting a mother.

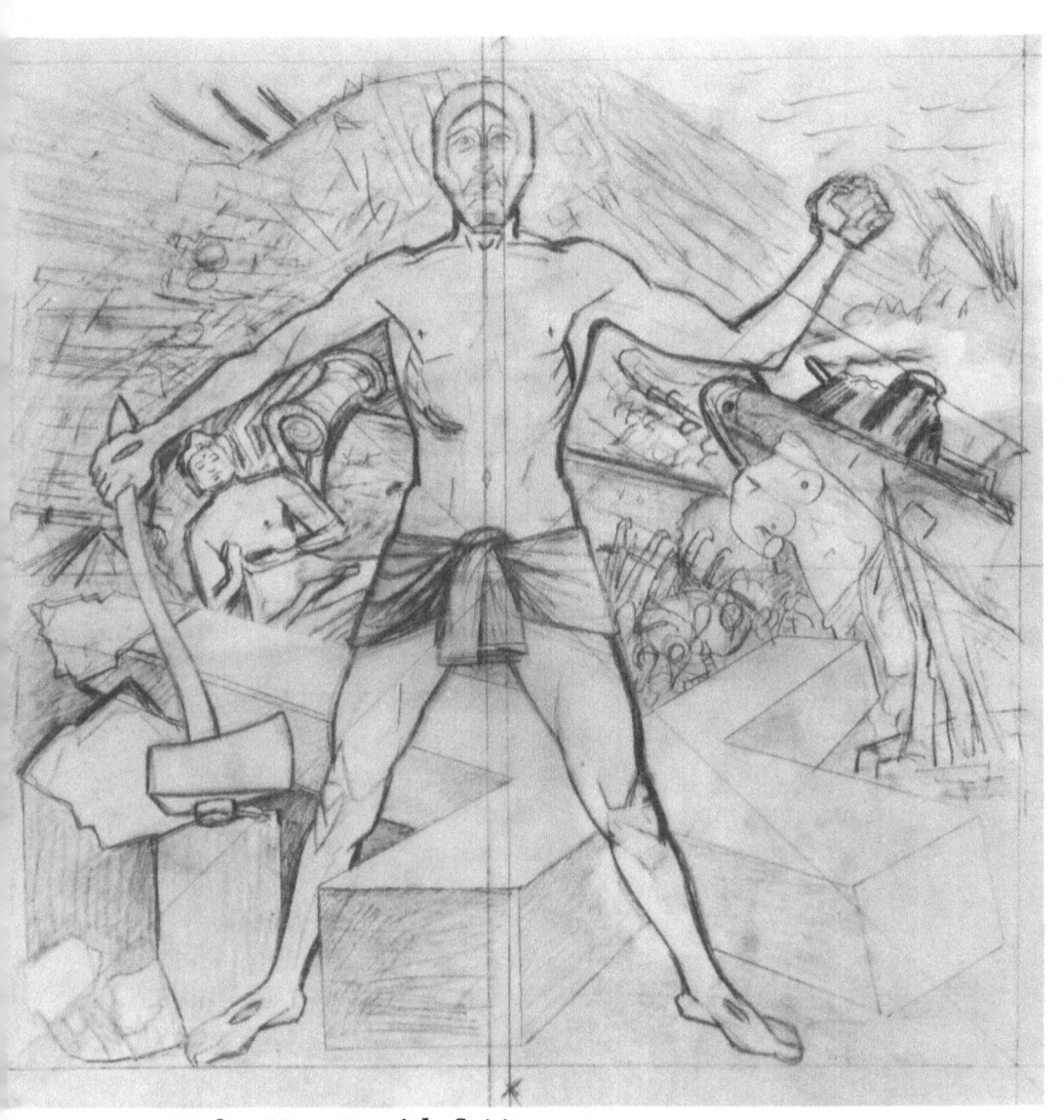

Modern Migration of the Spirit.

When Vasconcelos resigned his post it was impossible to go on working any longer. Siqueiros and I were driven out by the students, who badly defaced our pictures with their clubs and knives and the stones they threw.

The Syndicate was of no help, for the members would not support our protest. We had not yet learned the technique of publicity; if we had understood it, we would have gone on working in spite of all opposition. This technique is simple: it begins with shouting that whoever dislikes our pictures is a reactionary, a decrepit bourgeois and a Fifth Columnist, and that the pictures themselves are the patrimony of the Workers, without bothering to explain which workers, or why. The next step is to burst out in insults against the world in general but especially against prominent persons. After this the scientific and philosophical profundities are safely dragged in, for the listeners understand them as little as we do. The resources of commercial advertising are most varied, all the way from distributing handbills to lettering the blue sky with smoke from an airplane. A very effective and impressive trick consists in linking one's own name, as if inadvertently and in passing, with that of a great man; for example, Aristotle, Charlemagne, myself, and Julius Caesar. Politics, too, affords inexhaustible resources: a biography, invented by the candidate himself, and full of fake anecdotes and episodes that never happened. In childhood he was most precocious and in adolescence he was most studious. He is a respected parent and a patriotic citizen who has sacrificed himself for the public good. His op-

118

ponent is a clown, a mass of evils, a creature of the dictatorship.

Next in order come the devices of the medicine man, with his famished, harmless snake which dances the conga and answers questions put to it by the worthy public. But first there is always time for the medicine man to dispose of a few dozen flasks of toothache medicine.

All this without counting modern publicity techniques at the service of whatever commodity: smiling "stars," bullfights, armaments, chewing gum, building sites in the Lomas and Acapulco, warships, socks, toasted sunflower seeds, international treaties, soft drinks, lottery tickets.

One effective method is to put in an appearance stark naked and stand on your head at the corner of San Juan de Letrán and Madero at midday.

If we had known this, neither Siqueiros nor I would have been driven out onto the street like mad dogs.

These scandals finished the Syndicate off.

Later I had the good fortune to make the acquaintance of Francis W. S. Iturbe, a man of exquisite culture, a gentleman who honored me with his friendship. Señor Iturbe commissioned me to do a fresco on the wall of the stairway landing in the House of Tiles, which is the property of the Iturbe family. The painting was entitled *Omniscience*. Somewhat later still, I returned to the Preparatory School to finish the work I had begun, this time under the invaluable protection of Dr. Alfonso Pruneda, then rector of the National University. To that date belong the stairway pictures and those of the third story, as well as a heroic feat of painting: for the Industrial School in Orizaba, by order of Dr. J. M. Puig Casauranc, Secretary of Education, I did a mural of some thousand square feet in only two weeks and with the help of a single mason only.

Between 1924 and 1926 the humbug of pulque-shop painting arose, the sublime manifestation of plastic genius in the Mexican people, the powerful, the immortal work of a cosmic race, a telluric convulsion, a throwback to ancestral cosmogonies, to divine creation, and so on. Poor pulque-shop paintings. They have disappeared without a trace, and not precisely because of some telluric convulsion but because they were painted with glue and paste. A few days ago in Colonia San Rafael I came upon a pulque shop under the sign of "The Tigers," and only the name would have led me to suppose they had tried to paint tigers. The effect was more that of mangy dogs, without charm, without a trace of originality. It would be useless to search through the city for examples of pulque-shop art. Not a one remains.

As for retables, there are some very interesting ones, some magnificent ones, even works of genius, but the rest are like pulque-shop painting, like the tiny figures that amateurs make the world over. The retables repeat the same theme over and over with little variation: the bed, the kneeling sick man, and the apparition in the clouds. Thanks to Surrealism these things have passed for works of art: something remotely resembling a chair is painted and labeled *Child Playing with His Dog*. There only remains to have it framed and, presto, there you are.

120

Chapter 12 My Second Visit to New York. Harlem. The Yiddish Theatre. Naples in New York. Alma Reed and Eva Sikelianos. And Sarojini Naidu. The Untouchables.

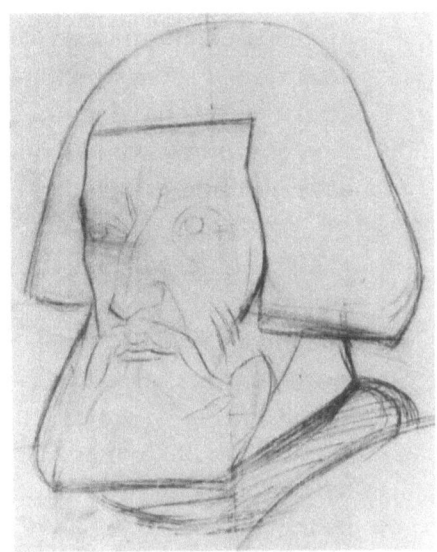

Head of Cortez from *Cortez and the Cross.*

𝒯here was little to hold me in Mexico in 1927, and I resolved to go to New York, counting upon generous support from Genaro Estrada, Secretary of Foreign Relations, who found the money to defray my journey and a stay of three months.

It was December, and very cold in New York. I knew nobody, and I proposed to begin all over. I found a comfortable room on Riverside Drive, a step or two from the Hudson and quite close to Columbia University. It was one

123

of the basement rooms with a short flight of stone steps up to an entrance at the street level. By night the snow would pile up in front of the door and block it completely, so that the next morning I would have to make a breach in the drift in order to emerge. I liked this labor, it made me happy.

My rambles took me up and down the river bank by day and into the many theatres, cabarets, and dancing halls of the immense district of Harlem by night. Negroes of stately carriage, some of them as black as the pulp of the black zapote. All of them tall and well set up. Some, the young women, mad to whiten their skin and straighten their kinky hair. Rich Negroes who indulge themselves in the luxury of hiring white domestics. Girls of vibrant features, strong, firm bodies, and an incredible beauty. Actresses and dancers like no others in the world. Powerful men who play and weep like children.

Other times I would make for the lower end of Manhattan, the Italian district, and the so-called "Ghetto." In this area were many theatres. A long and complicated comedy was playing in one of them, with too many characters and in the Yiddish tongue. But the action, the costumes, and the settings made it clear: the elder son of a Jewish family had fallen under the spell of a Catholic priest, who was done in caricature and all covered with crosses, front and back, from head to foot. The boy was on the point of turning Christian, and his family were making frantic efforts to save him. A

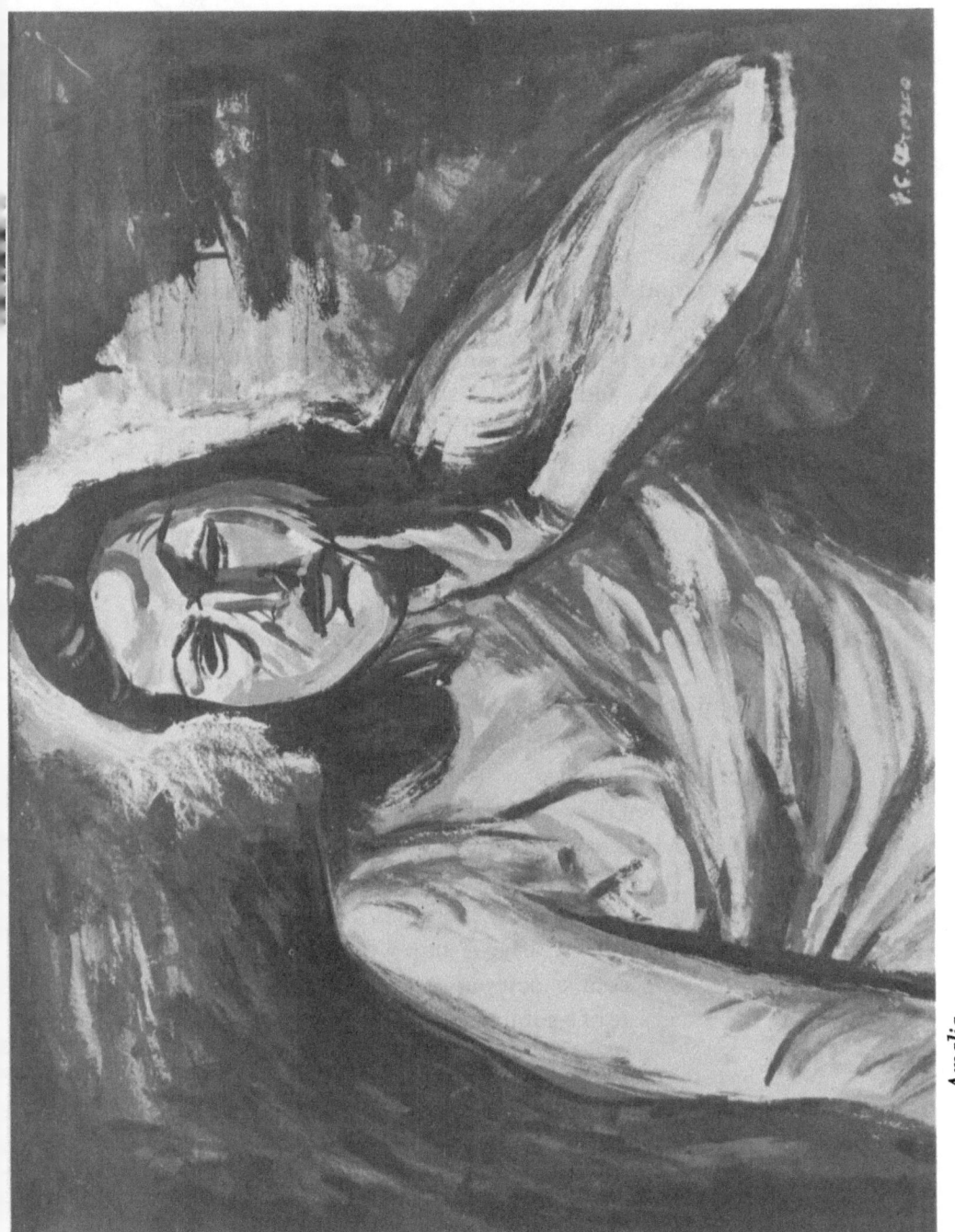

Amalia.

grand finale, with the youth in repentant flight from the priest, the family rejoicing, and the audience weeping and embracing one another. Submerged, all of this, in a dense, hot atmosphere and the fumes of tobacco.

Close to the Jewish district is a populous Italian one, larger than Naples. Family parties, in the street, with phonographs. Wandering tumblers to entertain the children. Up above, crossing the street from window to window, clotheslines hung with the drying wash. Puppet shows with their rude dramas and truculent tragedies of love, betrayal, and jealousy in formidable castles guarded by giants armed with lances and huge scimitars. Othello and Desdemona, Aïda, the *Divine Comedy*, Boccaccio. Then the lunch room with its interminable macaroni, stupendous broccoli, and red wine. The fantastic variety of Italian cheeses in the dairies. A sumptuous wedding with the married couple followed by hundreds of relatives and wandering musicians in wreaths.

In Greenwich Village I visited Carlos Chávez in his tiny little house with the grand piano.

It is only a two minutes' walk from Italy to China or Japan. In Chinatown they celebrate the New Year in the middle of our year, to the undulating advance of a paper dragon in a painted mantle, a monster three blocks long. The crackle and bang of fireworks. Chop suey and lobster. In the Japanese restaurant they serve a soup which is like the bottom of the sea: corals, octopus, starfish, snails. Farther down, the wreckage of a submarine.

126

Ladies I had known in Mexico introduced me to Alma Reed. Alma Reed had been in Mexico to write some articles on archeology for the New York *Times*. In Yucatán she had met the Governor, Felipe Carrillo Puerto, and falling in love they planned to marry. While she was on her way home to prepare for the wedding, Carrillo Puerto was assassinated in the outbreak of the De la Huerta revolt. His heartbroken fiancée was now on the point of embarking for Europe, where she would devote herself to archeological investigations in Italy and Greece. In the latter country she had known Eva Sikelianos, wife of the tragic poet Angelo Sikelianos, who with her support was the inspiration behind a Greek nationalist movement having for its purpose nothing less than the renaissance of ancient Greek culture.

Sikelianos' poems were works of genius of a lofty order, and Alma Reed set to work to translate them into English. When I met her, she and Mme. Sikelianos were living in a spacious house on lower Fifth Avenue. They had come to New York to solicit financial support for the cause of Greek resurgence and to organize excursions to the biennial festivals in Delphos. In 1929 *Prometheus Bound* and *The Suppliants* would be presented in the ancient Delphic theatre itself. There was also a promise of Olympic Games in the stadium, exhibitions of popular art, and songs and dances of shepherds from Parnassus.

Mme. Sikelianos' literary and revolutionary salon was constantly thronged. One day Greeks would come, among them Dr. Kalimacos, Patriarch of the Greek Orthodox

127

Church in New York. One heard the purest of modern Greek from the lips of the hostesses. Another day there would be Hindus, bronze-faced and turbaned, devoted followers of Mahatma Gandhi. Sarojini Naidu, in the costume of her country, the distinctive red mark of her high caste between her brows, would make her majestic entrance, followed by a train of young ladies and secretaries, these likewise in their colorful and gold-bordered dresses and veils. Mme. Naidu, a fellow worker with Gandhi, had been educated at Oxford and spoke excellent English. She was heading a committee to aid and publicize the Hindu people in passive resistance. Their arms were to be household looms upon which they would weave their own clothes in defiance of the laws which protected cloth imported from England; and the people had already rebelled *en masse* against the state monopoly in salt and were going down to the sea to make salt for themselves.

A brilliant spokesman for the suffering people of India was an elegant young lecturer who, it was said, was directly descended from Mahomet, which quite bowled the ladies over. Once he delivered a series of magnificent lectures, thoroughly documented and most instructive, upon comparative religion.

Other evenings, purely literary, were chiefly attended by Americans, and these in greater part aristocratic ladies, from whom in particular support for the Greek and the Hindu cause was expected. Alma Reed would recite her translations from Sikelianos' epic poems, some of which had appeared in a volume entitled *Dedication*. One of them, with a reference to "A new generation of gods," sounded splendid. After this came some grandiose rhythms by Van Noppen, a Dutch poet who was writing a poem of cosmic proportions. Last of all, the ladies in the gathering were indulgently permitted to bring out their own ingenuous and simple compositions. They were delighted and they modestly asked to be criticized sincerely, but they were simply applauded in every case.

The story of Van Noppen, who has disappeared, is a pitiful one. He was a poet of genuine talent, but he was shy and pusillanimous. The ladies would keep suggesting changes, corrections of his versification and additions to it and even to his ideas, and he would agree, so that he never did hit upon a definitive form.

Mme. Sikelianos, Mme. Naidu and Miss Reed were deeply interested in my paintings and sketches of the Revolution, and these were hung and exhibited on the walls of the drawing-room. Mme. Naidu in particular felt for the unfortunate Mexican peons in their struggle against injustice, and believed that their plight was similar to that of millions and millions of untouchables in her own land; but she was informed that the most wretched of Mexican laborers was immensely fortunate in comparison with those poor creatures in India, whose condition is inferior to that of the filthiest animal in the way they are utterly deprived of human, civil, and political rights; deprived of the right to work even, to gain an education, to move freely about, to speak, to complain; obliged to burn the widow alive on the corpse of the husband; victims of frightful diseases, starving, help-less, plunged in corruption, with no hope but to die. Such is their state that people of a higher caste may not even touch them. They *are* untouchable.

Chapter 13

I Become a Greek. Laurel Wreaths. The Crash. Surrealistic Economy. The Delphic Studios. The Tsar of Russia's Clock. Pomona and Prometheus. Home, Sweet Home.

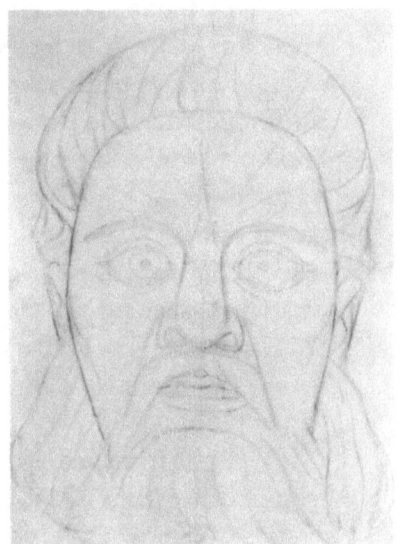

Head of Quetzalcoatl from *The Coming of Quetzalcoatl.*

 mong the objects of Greek folk art with which Mme. Sikelianos' house was profusely decorated was homespun, and the resemblance of this to certain modern serapes in gray, white, and black was remarkable. The setting was consequently a happy one for my sketches from the Revolution, most of which represented incidents in the clashes of Zapatistas, Villistas, and Carrancistas.

To my Greek friends it seemed that their

133

people of today have characteristics in common with the Mexican, just as the two countries bear a certain physical resemblance to each other. Alma Reed, who knew Mexico, confirmed this: the same primitivism, the same good taste in shaping and coloring objects of daily use, the same ferocity in defense of liberty. Photographs of Greek farmers standing with their burros in front of their huts might have been taken for photographs of Mexicans. Very likely this was what won me the friendship of Mme. Sikelianos and Dr. Kalimacos. In their sympathy they went so far as to confer an exceptional and unmerited honor upon me.

One night I was invited to Van Noppen's house on Staten Island, along with all of our Greek friends. Alma Reed recited Sikelianos' Delphic words from "Prologue to Life," "Calypso," "Resurrection," and fragments of his tragedies *The Sibyl, Daedalos* and *Asclepios,* works, all of them, in the Aeschylean line. Then Dr. Kalimacos rose and solemnly declared: to the Greeks, all true artists the world over, of whatever period, are Greeks. Van Noppen and I bowed our heads, and Dr. Kalimacos crowned us with laurel wreaths and bestowed new names upon us. I was rebaptized with the name of Panselenos, that is, of a famous Greek painter of Byzantine times whose murals are to be found in Mistra. On this occasion the laurel wreath was not precisely a symbol of triumph but of adoption. Immortal Greece had deemed us worthy to enter her studios as the lowliest and most backward of apprentices.

The night was clear, the moon was bright, and as I re-

134

turned to Manhattan on the ferry boat, across the enchanted bay of New York, my imagination was full of the elongated, rigid, austere images of the Apostles and the Virgin at the feet of the gigantic Pantocrat.

The whole Hellenic community harbored great contempt for Rome. To them Greece alone was the creator of beauty; Rome was monstrous, hard, heavy, the home of slaves and despots. But this was no impediment to Mme. Sikelianos' having for one of her best friends a splendid Roman princess whom we used to visit in her elegant residence. In the princess' great salon there were neither chairs nor divans but the floor was strewn with superb bearskins and cushions on which the ladies would rest their white and perfumed and silk-shrouded bodies.

One morning in 1929 something very serious was happening in New York. People were rushing about even more than usual and wherever a group gathered the discussion was hysterical. Fire trucks and Red Cross sirens shrieked madly on every side, and the extras, great bundles of which were fetched on trucks, flew from hand to hand. Wall Street and the neighborhood were a raging sea of activity. Many speculators had already leaped from their office windows, and their bodies were gathered up by the police. Office boys no longer bet on whether the boss would commit suicide but on whether he would do it before or after lunch. Thousands and thousands of people lost their money and whatever else they possessed in a matter of minutes. Stock-market values dropped to zero. What had been a fortune turned into a

135

frightful debt. The Crash. Overproduction and failure to export. World markets filled with goods that no one bought. Factories closed and immense negotiations at a standstill. Panic. Suspended credit. A rise in the cost of living. Millions suddenly laid off, and the numerous employment agencies on Sixth and Seventh Avenues vainly stormed by the jobless. Those in power had promised endless prosperity and a chicken in every pot, but now there was not even a fire on millions of hearths. The municipality found itself obliged to open soup kitchens, and in the outlying districts there were frightening lines of powerful men queued up, hatless, in old clothes that offered little protection through hours of subzero weather as they stood on the frozen snow. Red-faced, hard, desperate, angry men, with opaque eyes and clenched fists. By night in the protection of the shadows, whole crowds begged in the streets for a nickel for coffee, and there was no doubt, not the slightest, that they needed it. This was the Crash. Disaster.

Overproduction brought prices down, and with them profits. To force prices back up, production was limited by reducing the acreage under cultivation and plowing cotton and potatoes under. Less mining and less industry. But this increased the number of the unemployed, and required the manufacture of more arms, with which to kill off the jobless and increase profits and executives' salaries. Then war broke out in Europe. Nations had recourse to the practice of the third-rate tenor who, whenever he sang a false note, would

136

Migration. Study for head of Aztec migrant.

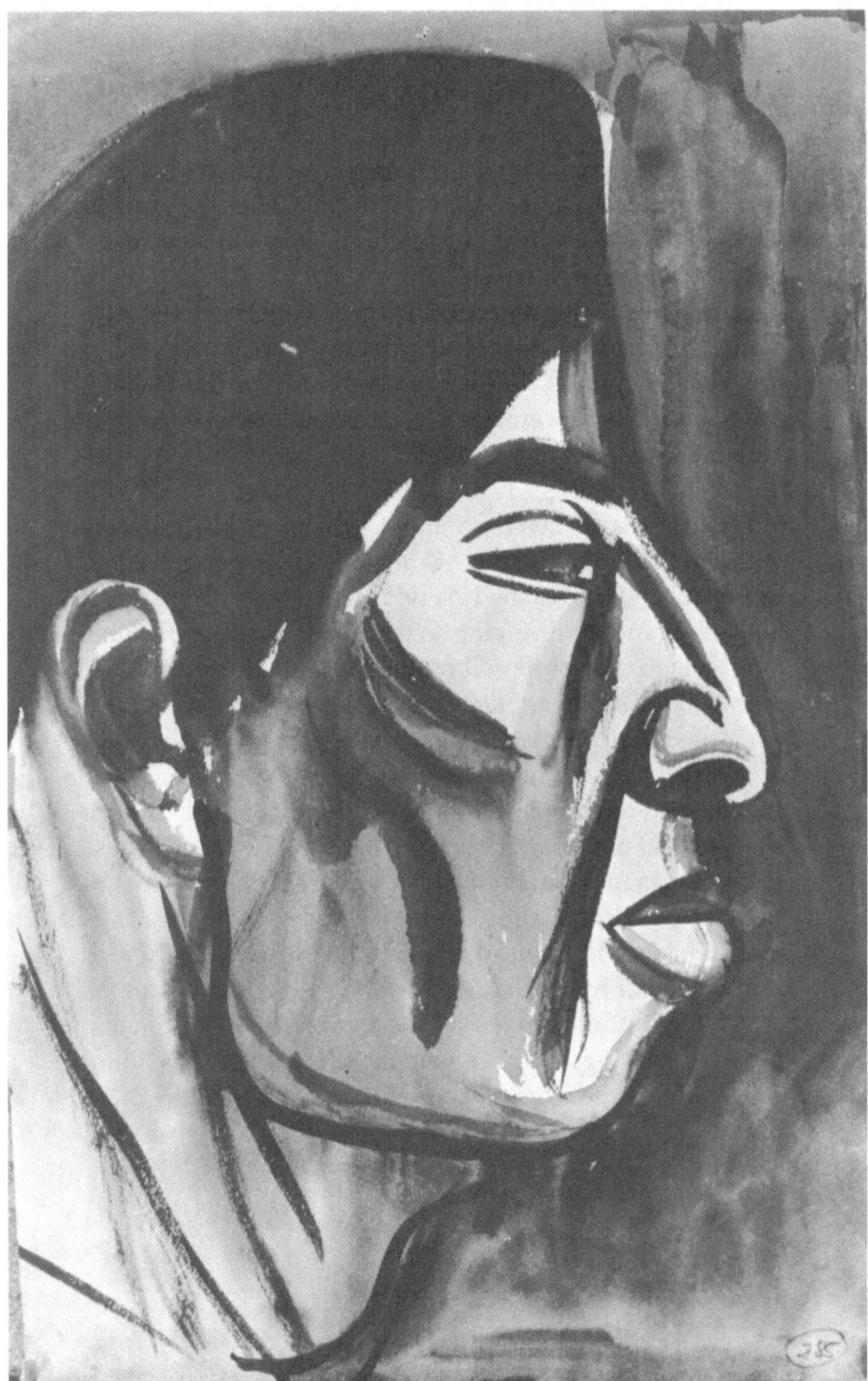

immediately shout "Viva, Mexico!" and pull the tricolor from his pocket.

Mme. Sikelianos sailed for Europe, where she had my Revolutionary sketches exhibited in the Gallery "Fermé la Nuit" in Paris. They had already been shown in New York, in Marie Sterner's gallery.

Alma Reed, who remained behind, conceived the gracious plan of a New York gallery for my work. I assented to this, deeply obliged, and it was established as the Delphic Studios, on Fifty-seventh Street, close to the most important New York galleries of painting.

When it was opened there appeared some White Russians who had fled from Moscow at the time of the Bolshevist triumph. They had reached New York by way of Shanghai and San Francisco, bringing an enormous quantity of works of art which they proposed to sell. Icons richly ornamented with gold and silver. Pictures, furniture, and incredibly sumptuous Chinese vases, along with ancient Persian rugs of every size and fantastic design; rare porcelains and ivories; and to complete the marvel objects that had been the personal property of the Tsar Nicholas II. Among these towered a monumental table clock, more than three feet in height, which, according to the inscription with its list of grand dukes and grand duchesses, his relatives had given him on one of his birthdays. It stood on a silver hillock on which a multitude of chubby little angels were cutting capers and playing tricks. In general effect it was heavy, insolent, and in the worst of taste. Little by little all the other objects in the lot disappeared into museums or private collections, but the Tsar's clock found no buyer. I had it in my bedroom for a long time and afterwards it accompanied me to Los Angeles, where I lost sight of it.

In 1930 my old friend Jorge Juan Crespo wrote from Hollywood to say that José Pijoan, Professor of the History of Art in Pomona College, wanted to have a Mexican painter decorate the walls of the College refectory. Jorge Juan had suggested my name and now he was inviting me to Pomona. I accepted and set out. To the trustees of the College the idea had not seemed a very good one, but the students and some of the professors were quite taken with it.

The refectory was a large building, capacious enough to house some two hundred diners in comfort. At one end was a fireplace and above it a wall surface of some thousand square feet.

The fee was trifling, made up of small contributions by students and professors. After deliberating, we agreed upon the theme of "Prometheus," and I began at once, to the disgust of the trustees, who would grumble as they made their way through the refectory and eye the scaffoldings askance, disposed to fall upon me at the first misstep.

Still, the work got done, and I went back to San Francisco —though with less money in my purse than when I arrived for the first time, in 1917. It was not even enough for my return passage to New York. I set about painting a picture, *Zapata Entering a Peasant's Hut*, which now hangs in the

139

Art Institute of Chicago. I made a poor bargain of selling it and recrossed the continent. When I reached Manhattan my heart was light with the joy and confidence of one who returns to his hearth—of skyscrapers, subways, and art. Home, Sweet Home.

Chapter 14 Painting in the School for Social Research. Dynamic Symmetry. The Secret of Beauty.

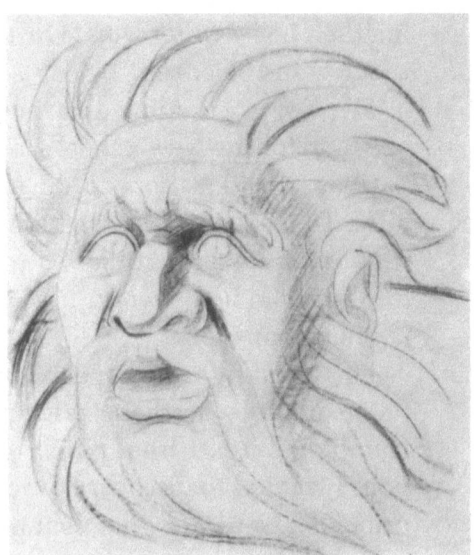

Head of Quetzalcoatl from *The Departure of Quetzalcoatl.*

In 1930 I painted frescoes on the walls of a hall in the modern building of the New School for Social Research.

The themes of the paintings are these. In the middle, the Table of Universal Brotherhood. People of all races presided over by a Negro. On the side walls, allegories of World Revolution. Gandhi. Carrillo Puerto and Lenin. Then a group of slaves and another of workers entering their houses after work. On a wall outside, an allegory of the Arts and Sciences.

The Negro presiding and the portrait of Lenin were the occasion for the New School's losing a number of its richest patrons, a serious loss to an institution dependent upon gifts. To make up for this, on the other hand, it gained the support of numerous other patrons. I had been given absolute freedom in my work: it was a school for investigation, not for submission.

This painting is of a special nature in being based upon the geometrico-aesthetic principles of the investigator Jay Hambidge. Apart from purely personal motives of expression, I wanted to discover how convincing and useful those principles were and what their possibility was.

Hambidge was an American geometer whose central idea was to discover the relations between art and the structure of natural forms in man and plants, and then, on a basis of historical data and direct measurements of temples, vases, statues, and jewels, to formulate an exact and scientific statement of the construction of objects of Hellenic art. He had begun his work in 1900, and afterwards he was supported by Yale University in investigations in Greece and in museums throughout Europe. He published a treatise, *Dynamic Symmetry;* an analysis of Greek temples: the Parthenon, the Temple of Apollo in Arcadia, that of Zeus in Olympia, and those in Aegina and in Sunium near Athens; a study of vases; and finally a review with the title *The Diagonal.*

Hambidge died around 1928 and his widow, Mary Ham-

144

bidge, whom I met in Mme. Sikelianos' salon, proposed that we should go on, she and I, with his unfinished work in vital structure, but it was out of the question for me to undertake such long and laborious studies, which would have kept me away from painting for a considerable time.

Hambidge's theories have a solid historical basis. According to inscriptions the Egyptians employed surveyors and topographers in orienting temples and tracing their ground plans. The measuring device was a rope divided into twelve equal parts by means of knots. After drawing a line with the Great Bear for a point of reference, they would determine a perpendicular by using the divisions in the rope, three of them and four of them respectively for the legs and five for the hypotenuse. The whole temple would have proportions reached in this way.

In the Theaetetus, where there is mention of rectangles derived from squares and their diagonals, Plato speaks of the incommensurability of certain roots. All this is at the beginning of the Dialogue. A geometer named Exodus, one of Plato's contemporaries, investigated the "Section," later known as the "Divine" or "Golden Section," which is nothing but the ratio between a shorter and a longer side of the rectangle 1.618 [1 by 0.618].

Euclid's propositions teach us to distinguish between an area with commensurate or rational lines on the one hand and one with incommensurate or irrational ones on the other.

Dynamic Symmetry is Hambidge's interpretation of the

145

Greek phrase "commensurate when raised in degree," the notion applied by Hellenic philosophers to the relations between the areas of "square root" rectangles, that is, of those figures having unity for the shorter sides and square root of two, three, four, or five for the longer ones.

According to the author of *Symmetry* there are two sorts of art: the dynamic and the static. To the first belong the arts of Greece and Egypt in their mature periods. To the second he relegated all other art without exception. The forms created by Greeks and Egyptians are dynamic because they structurally comprise in themselves the principle of action, of movement, and for this reason can grow, develop, and multiply like the human body and all living beings. When this development is normal it produces rhythm and harmony, which are precisely what we mean by beauty. In this lies the supremacy of Greek and Egyptian art over all others.

Static art—Arabic, Chinese, Japanese, Hindu, Assyrian, Byzantine, Gothic, and so on—corresponds to the structure of inanimate matter, to crystals and the like. It is static because its elements are fixed and without the possibility of further development except for the exterior addition of elements equally passive.

The structure of dynamic forms consists of commensurate surfaces organized in geometrical proportion and has the square and its diagonal and the diagonal of half the square as a base or origin. From these diagonals the square-root

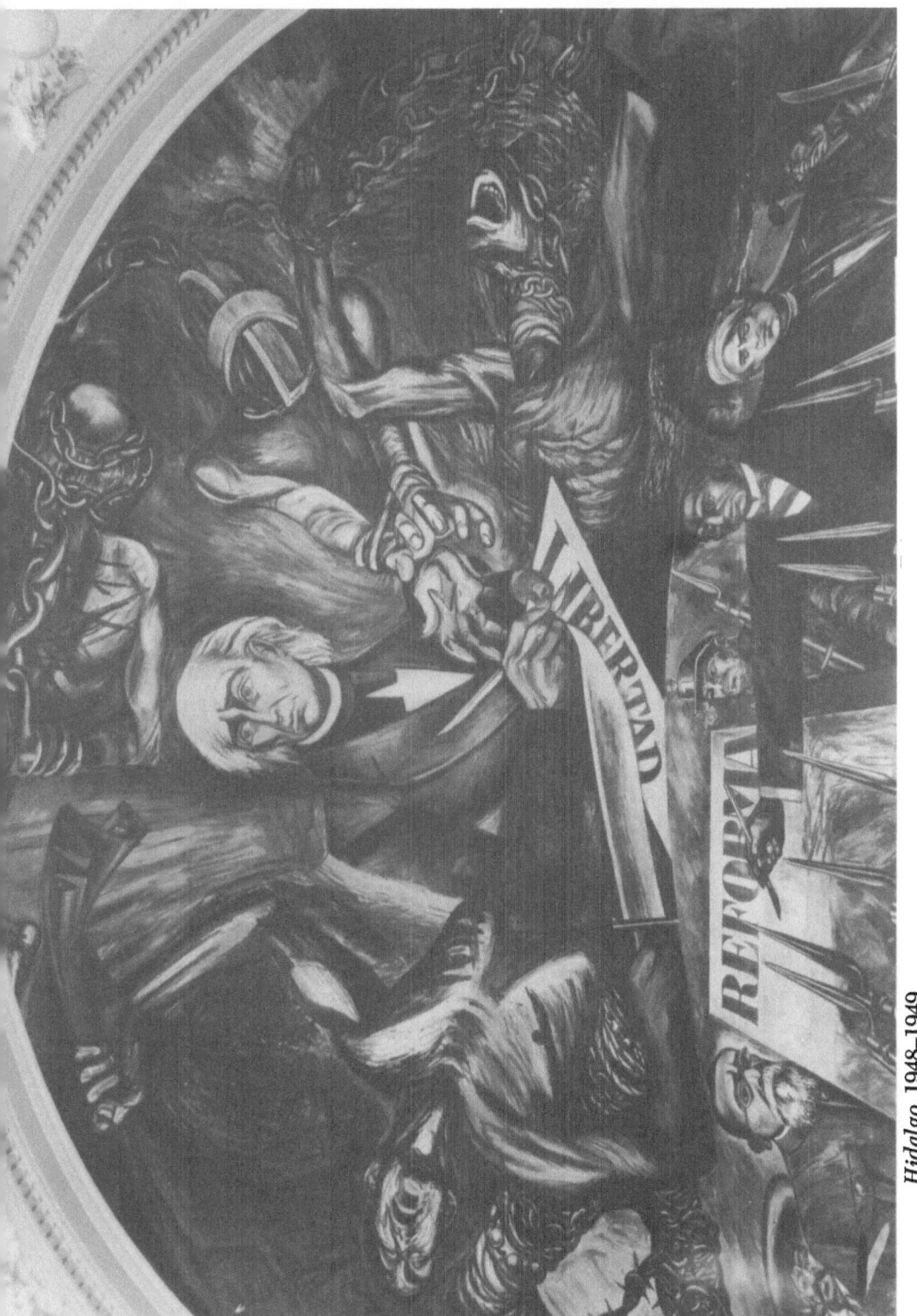

Hidalgo. 1948–1949.

rectangles are derived and from these in turn an infinite number of other rectangles.

It would be interesting to learn to which of the two types pre-Cortesian Art corresponds, especially the Toltec, the Aztec, and the Mayan. Hambidge maintains that dynamic art can exist only consciously and where created after a precise geometrical plan; he admits, though, that in true works of art the dynamic elements have appeared spontaneously, owing to the intuition or genius of the artist. This applies to all the arts without exception: painting, sculpture, architecture, music, literature, and the dance.

The Romans had no notion at all of the dynamic principles discovered and used by the Greeks. At most they suspected these principles. It was for this reason that Vitruvius, architect to the Age of Augustus, fell into the error of declaring that Hellenic statues and temples were brought into proportion by a "module," and the error persisted throughout the Middle Ages and was passed on to the Renaissance and thence to the academies, even in our times. Not a single example of Hellenic art corresponds to Vitruvius' modules; and equally absurd are the rules for constructing the human form as seven and a half or eight heads in height, to say nothing of the belief that a man's stature is equal to the distance from hand to hand when the arms are outstretched. In no more than a case out of twenty or thirty will these proportions be found. Vitruvius' modules have produced only static art: they are commensurate lengths, not surfaces. Along with this, since the Italian Renaissance, a plague of anatomy has soiled art down to the present. In other words there never was a Renaissance in so far as the plastic arts are concerned. There was only another and different art.

Dynamic Symmetry created a furor in the United States and Europe between 1920 and 1930. Not a painter, sculptor, architect, or decorator but endeavored to apply Hambidge's methods to his work. Still, as always happens, the principles were ill interpreted or turned into an academic rule. People imagined that at last the secret of Greek beauty had been uncovered, that it was at the service of anyone in possession of a compass or a foot rule who could add or divide. It was strange to see artists begin a picture or a carving like an accountant striking a balance in a bank, by making a long series of calculations. The only result of this was a notable improvement in the decorative arts. Woven stuffs, furniture, tapestries, books, and ceramics took on a different and better look. Hambidge himself carried his conclusions too far, but he did the arts a service in providing them with an instrument without which they cannot survive, a very old but forgotten instrument: geometry.

Modern art had forgotten Dynamic Symmetry, but it could not dispense with geometry, for its capital preoccupation was the objective form. It reached this empirically, intuitively, there being no other possible road. Surrealism itself, however far it may stray into dreams, has need of forms, which must be dynamic, since otherwise the dream turns into death. The beautiful, for man, is only what is built like his own body, his spirit.

After doing the pictures in the New School I abandoned the overrigorous and scientific methods of Dynamic Symmetry, but I kept what was fundamental and inevitable in it and with this I shaped new ways of working. I had the explanation of many former errors and I saw new roads opening up.

Chapter 15 Raphael's Cartoons—London, Paris, Italy, and Spain. Dartmouth College.

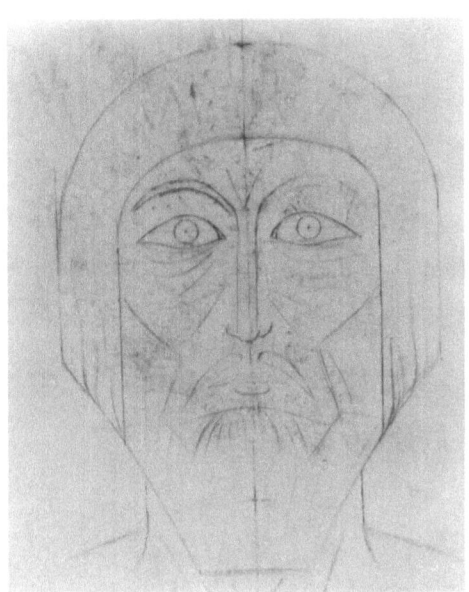

Head of Christ from *Modern Migration of the Spirit.*

In 1932 I went to Europe, a visit of three months only. I had no plan of getting to know it—ninety days is too short a time for that. I merely wanted to see a part of the great paintings in museums and churches.

The first city I visited was London, since I had heard admiring talk of the cartoons or sketches that Raphael did for the tapestries in the Vatican. I heard that some very famous Chinese artists had been in Europe getting to

153

know all the museums. When they were afterwards asked which work was in their opinion the best of what they had seen, they said it was these cartoons. So on arriving I went directly to the Albert and Victoria Museum of Industrial Arts, and I saw for myself that the Chinese artists were right. The cartoons are some twelve or fourteen in number, I don't remember exactly which. They are approximately ten by thirteen feet in dimensions and are painted on paper or some fine cloth that resembles paper. They seem to be water colors and their colors are most brilliant. The composition is rich and sumptuous. They are so impressive that they could well be superior to the same master's frescoes and paintings in the Vatican. It was regrettable to find them hung very high in a dim hall, which kept one from appreciating the details.

London was like the seat of a noble family which had been exceedingly rich but had lost its fortune. Everything grown dim. A lack of repairs. Wreckage. Many of the benches covered with elaborate sketches in color, and over each sketch a man working, his palette in hand, his hat ostentatiously placed to catch alms from the compassionate public. There was no street without such artists. I had formed a different picture of London. Who could expect this of a country which was mistress of all the seas and had such colonies as Canada, India, Australia, and half of Africa; which dominates world finance, and once possessed all the oil, all the rubber, all the waterfalls? I would never have imagined that I, a citizen of a modest and, as they say, semi-

154

colonial country, would come to be distributing alms to the hungry in the streets and squares of the capital of England.

I saw a Paris that was old, ruined, miserable. Where could the elegant and beautiful women be? In the course of a month I saw not one, not a single one. After six in the evening Paris is an immense brothel. Thousands and thousands of prostitutes sitting at the tables in the cafés, and thousands more prowling through the streets in ferocious search of passersby. But worst of all was the incredible number of men shamelessly making vile proposals. The neighborhood of the "Follies" full of bookshops exhibiting the "literature" of the subject and the most shameless pictures. Old, old Montmartre a moldering cadaver, and Montparnasse full of vagabonds and the dispirited. Clearly, all this wretchedness was not France; ancient and beloved France was another matter. What I was seeing was very likely a hoax to divert the tourists, who invade Europe in great hordes, expecting to see what their guide books tell them they will see. In the harbors the ships that arrived from the three Americas unload their happy average complements of passengers with itineraries clearly defined, measured, calculated to the minute in advance. With exact instructions as to what to see, hear, smell, taste, touch, think, and feel.

All over Europe the same thing happens. When the tourists arrive in the spring the inhabitants of picturesque places arrange their fraudulent stage settings in the very streets, don the garb of a century ago and expose the stores of furniture and other objects described in novels. When winter comes they strip their houses of the patina of age and return their costumes, their ornaments, and their typical old carriages to the storeroom. The theatre is put away for the next year.

Far from being such fiction was a great retrospective showing of Picasso in the Gallery George Petit; equally far from it were the sensational newspaper exposures, documented beyond dispute, of the shameful politicians and the dealers in cannon fodder. Exposures of how Germany and the Allies had exchanged critical materials during the progress of the First World War and so prolonged that war in the interests of big speculators. There was no fiction, either, in the sidewalk exhibitions of photographs showing soldiers who lived on with their faces partly or completely shot away. They were left with the bare possibility of breathing or of sustaining life on predigested foods poured directly into their alimentary tracts through special tubes. Philanthropists could boast of having supplied them with masks which gave them a human appearance. Others had lost not only their faces but arms and legs, and miraculously went on living, transformed into beings which beggared the most lurid artistic imagination.

After I had admired the wonders of the British Museum and the National Gallery, I saw El Greco's great Christ in the Louvre, where with its geometric simplicity it dominates a hall of the giants among artists. Then the gala springtides of Claude Monet. Napoleon in Les Invalides.

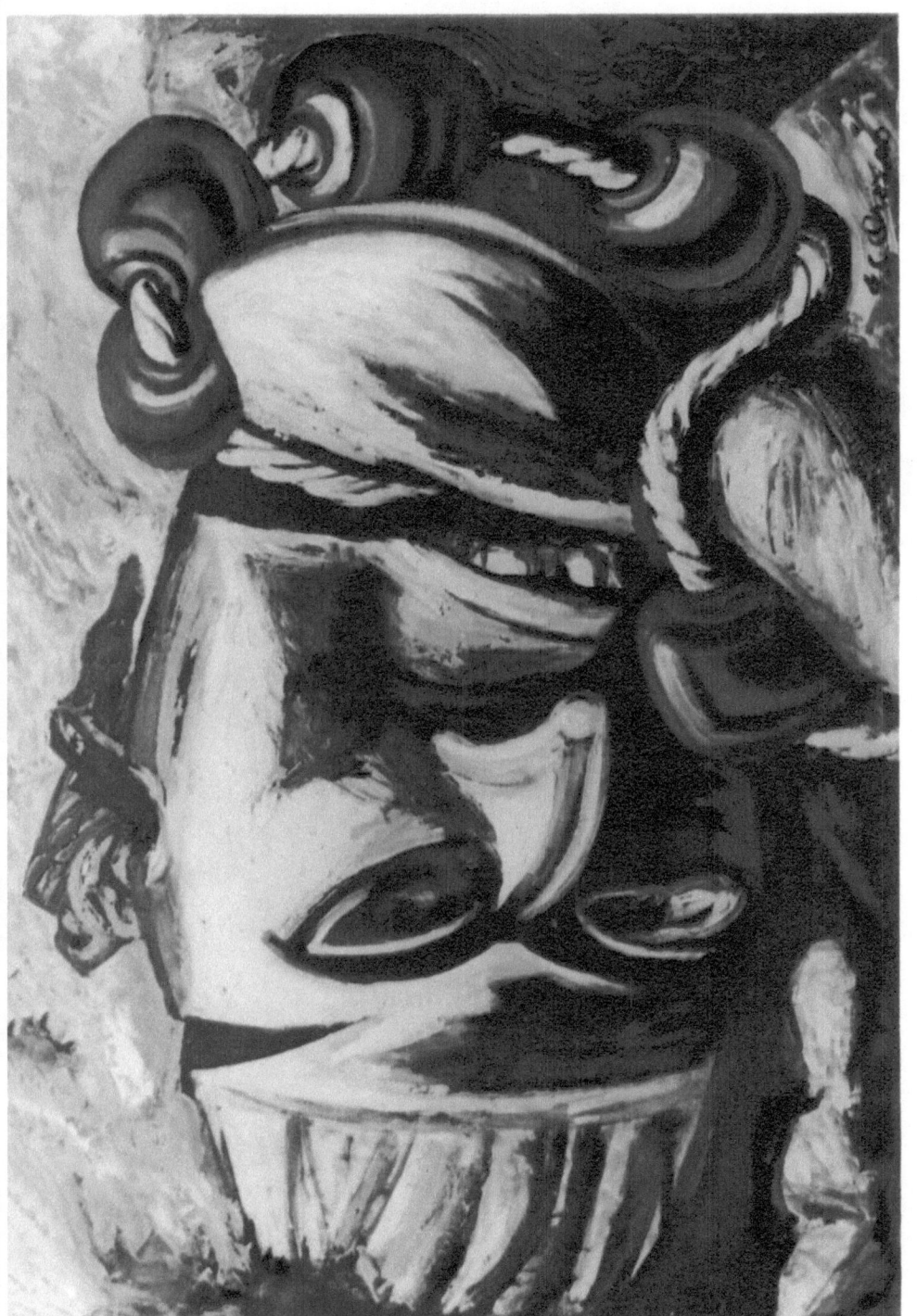

Mask with Jade Necklace.

I entered Italy by way of the Simplon and stopped in Milan to see Leonardo's *Last Supper*. In Padua, Giotto. In Venice, Titian, Tintoretto, St. Mark's. Then Ravenna and Florence, where I encountered Don José Pijoan on his way to Switzerland. In a day-long lesson he took me to see Santa María del Fiore, the great Florentines and the Uffizi. Assisi, Arezzo. Rome—the Sistine and the immense museums of the Vatican! The Appian Way and the Catacombs. The Baths. The Coliseum. Naples, after seeing which you can die. Pompeii and its Villa of Mysteries, in which I learned much, much, of the art of painting. The streets of the dead city and the bodies still imprisoned in lava. The frescoes and mosaics in the houses and the shops. Turning north, Rome again. Pisa and Genoa. By rail to Marseilles. Then Barcelona, Saragossa, Madrid, Toledo, and Avila. In Toledo they are still burying the Count of Orgaz, and El Greco still lives and paints, and his Apostles still work by the day. One of them carries my baggage to the hotel, another serves me a glass of wine, that one yonder is the driver of the Madrid bus, and I see still another on the Bridge of Alcántara. San Sebastián, Paris once more, and in Le Havre I embark. Six days of perfect rest upon a blue and green and violet, a warm and tranquil, Atlantic. New York.

Dartmouth College in Hanover, New Hampshire, is one of the oldest of educational institutions in the American Union. Several years before the War of Independence it was founded by a missionary who wished to educate the Indians of the neighborhood. Eleazar Wheelock came among them with a grammar, a Bible, a drum, and more than five thousand quarts of whiskey. To the sound of his drum, the Indians assembled, drank his whiskey, and learned the idiom of the New Testament. Today there are no more Indians left to be educated after this admirable plan. The College preserves Wheelock's grammar, his Bible, and his drum. It now has great halls, stadiums, and laboratories, which are worth millions of dollars. In the midst of it all stands Baker Library, the pride of the College, with a collection of books in Spanish which by itself is greater than many very important libraries in Spanish America.

On the ground floor of the library I painted a series of murals for the Department of Fine Arts, whose Director was Mr. Artemas Packard.

My stay in Dartmouth, from 1932 to 1934, was altogether agreeable and satisfactory. Dartmouth is one of the best examples of Liberalism in the North, and of New England hospitality. New Englanders are completely different from other groups of Americans. Country folk, hostile and formal in their dealings with outlanders and new arrivals, but most cordial on closer acquaintance, and anxious to be neighborly, to understand one, and to help out with the greatest good will, disinterest, and courtesy.

The Administration and the 2500 students of the College were enthusiastic in their support of the Fine Arts project, and so I set to work.

I had complete freedom to express my ideas; no suggestion or criticism of any sort was ever made.

In the beginning there had been some opposition to the

158

idea of a foreigner's painting the walls of an institution which is one of the sanctuaries of that Idealism upon which the great country of the North was founded. But the protests came from Boston, not Hanover. Many of them bore signatures heavy with the difficult consonants of Central Europe, and those who signed protested in the name of one-hundred-percent Americanism, without comprehending that precisely the position Dartmouth was taking expressed one of the most highly prized of American virtues: freedom —of speech and thought, of conscience and the press—the freedoms of which the American people have always been justifiably proud.

The murals consist of fourteen pictures of approximately ten by thirteen feet in dimension, and ten smaller ones.

In the first of them the theme is that of "Quetzalcoatl," but the final paintings bear no very clear relation to this.

Dartmouth is delicious in winter. It stands on the Connecticut River, surrounded by forest-covered mountains.

In February a famous Carnival is held which attracts young ladies from the most aristocratic women's colleges and, Dartmouth being a school for men only, they are joyfully entertained in dances and skating parties.

One of the most important events in the winter fiesta is a competition in ice sculpture. The students are most skilful in erecting figures, and even monuments of great size. Each fraternity erects its own in front of the fraternity house and illuminates it by night. The effect is stupendous. While there I was a member of the jury to award prizes for these figures.

Sports are very important at Dartmouth, especially skiing in winter and football in summer.

When I had finished my work, faculty and students bade me a most cordial farewell.

Toward the end of 1934 I was back in Mexico. Antonio Castro Leal had entrusted me with the task of doing a painting for the Palace of Fine Arts, which was soon to be opened.

In 1936 I went to Guadalajara, where I was to remain for four years, engrossed in intense and fruitful labor.

INDEX

Academy of San Carlos: Orozco's training at, xix, 9, 10–12, 19; directors of, 10, 21, 30, 38; teaching techniques at, 10–12, 19, 30, 38; value of, 12; decay of, 26, 38; exhibit at, 28; and student strikes, 30–34; manifestos against, 33; and Revolution, 50

Acevedo (actor): as mimic, 45–46

Acosta, Manuel Becerra: and *The Vanguard*, 52, 53

advertising: techniques of, 118–119

Agriculture, School of (San Jacinto): Orozco's education at, 9

Ahuizote: descendants of, 29–30

Aïda: in puppet show, 126

Albert and Victoria Museum of Industrial Arts: Raphael cartoons in, 154–155

Alcalde, Carlos: and Orozco, 10

Amador Siqueiros, Graciela: 71, 113–114

Americanism: nature of, 159

Appian Way: Orozco at, 157

Apollo, Temple of: analysis of, 144

Arabs: 107

Archeology, Museum of: and Charlot, 87

architecture: and Europe, 20

Arezzo (artist): paintings of, 157

Argenteuil, France: 92

Arroyo, Vanegas: as printer, 8

art: and politics, xxi, 30; in United States, 66; democracy in, 76–77; Mexican thought on, 82; and sociology, 82; and history, 82; and society, 85, 99; and statesmen, 86; socialization of, 93; influence of, 96; and revolution, 96; as propaganda, 96; content of, 98; and the collectivity, 98–99; individualism in, 98–99; and geometry, 144–149; and Dynamic Symmetry, 149

—, indigenous: reverence for, 82; influences of, 87; preservation of, 109; and Jay Hambidge's theories, 148

—, Mexican: revolution in, 19–21; influence of Europe on, xvii, 19–20, 87, 92–93; exhibit of, 28; Infantilism in, xvii, 76–77, 82; and indigenous art, 82; nationalism in, 82

—, pre-Cortesian. SEE art, indigenous

—, proletarian: nature of, 93–94

—, revolutionary: of Siqueiros, 93

Art Institute of Chicago: Orozco's painting in, 139–140

Artistic Center: organization of, 29

arts and sciences: and frescoes, 143–144

Asclepios: of Angelo Sikelianos, 134

Assisi: Orozco in, 157

161

162

165

New Englanders: nature of, 158

New School for Social Research frescoes: xviii–xix, 143–144; themes of, 143–144; effect of, 144; principles of, 144

newspapers, American: on Orozco, 40

New York: state of art in, 66; Orozco in, 66–67, 71–75, 123–139, 157; Orozco's fondness for, 140

Niagara Falls: Orozco at, 66

Noche Triste: 107

Obregón, Alvaro: as revolutionary leader, 49–50; and Pancho Villa, 50; and Dr. Atl, 51, 53

Occidente: xvii, 3

Olaguíbel, Juan: 71–72, 72

Olavarrieta (philanthropist): Dr. Atl's portrait of, 19

Olympic Games: at Delphos, 127

Omniscience: by Orozco, 119

Ordorica, Miguel: as editor, 29

Orgaz, Count of: burying of, 157

Orozco, Clemente: nature of, xvii–xviii, xxi–xxii; education of, xviii, 7–10; murals by, xviii–xix, xx, xxii, 29, 118–119, 120, 139, 143–144, 158–159, 160; training of, xix, 9, 10–12, 19; style of, xix, xx–xxi; compared with other artists, xix, xx, xxi, xxii; influences on, xix, xx, 8–9, 12; at Academy of San Carlos, xix, 9, 10–12, 19; political philosophy of, xix, xxi, 30; and Alma Reed, xx, 127, 129, 138; as political cartoonist, xx, 29–30; on other artists, xx, 11, 25–26, 33, 86–87; youth of, 7–10; and Carlos Alcalde, 10; subjects painted by, 21, 30, 40, 60, 103, 119, 133, 139, 143–144, 159; showings of pictures by, 28, 138; first studio of, 38–40; revolutionary experiences of, 40–46, 50–51, 51–52, 53–56; colors used by, 40; loss of hand by, 40–41; and *The Vanguard,* 52–53; and Fernando R. Galván, 60, 62–65; in San Francisco, 60–66; in Canada, 66; in New York, 66–67, 71–75, 123–129; and *The Machete,* 114; and Eva Sikelianos, 129, 133, 134, 138; and the Greeks, 134; and Dr. Kalimacos, 134; in Europe, 153–157

Orozco, Margarita: xvii

Othello: in puppet show, 126

"Over There": singing of, 61

Orizaba: revolution in, 51–52, 53–56; Industrial School murals in, 120

Packard, Artemas: 158

Padua: Orozco in, 157

painters, mural: as a group, 85; influences on, 87; nature of, 88; themes of, 103

Painters and Sculptors, Syndicate of. SEE Syndicate of Painters and Sculptors

painting, new national school of: xviii

—, pulque-shop: xix, 120

—, types of: xix, 93, 98–99, 120

paints. SEE colors

Palace of Fine Arts: Orozco in, 160

Palavicini, Felix P.: 53

Panselenos: as Orozco's name, 134

Paris: influence of, on Mexican art, 19–20, 87; donkey's masterpiece

in, 77–78; description of, 155;
Orozco in, 157
Parthenon: analysis of, 144
passive resistance: in India, 128
peons, Mexican: plight of, 129
Peralvillo District: 45
Petit, George: and Picasso, 156
Petroleum Workers of Tampico: 114
Philosophy and Letters, Faculty of:
location of, 7–8
Phoenicians: 107
Picasso, Pablo: compared with
Orozco, xx; show of, 156
Pijoan, José: 139, 157
Pillet System: 30
Piña, Joaquín: 29, 60
Pisa: Orozco in, 157
Pissarro, Camille: influence of, 38
Plato: on geometry, 145
politics: Orozco on, xix, xxi; and
art, xxi, 30; nature of, 54;
advertising in, 118–119
Pomona: frescoes at, xviii–xix, 139
Pompeii: Orozco at, 157
Ponce, Manuel M.: 85
Pope, the: and usurpers, 41
Popocatépetl: Dr. Atl on, 21
Portuguese: racial extraction of, 107
Posada, José Guadalupe: xx, 8, 8–9
Preparatory School: xviii, 10
—, murals: 29; painting of, 116–118;
student reaction to, 116, 117;
public reaction to, 116; finishing
of, 118–119
primitivism. SEE Infantilism
Prince of Wales: in Canada, 66
proletarian: 93–94, 94, 96
proletarian art: nature of, 93–94

"Prologue to Life": 134
"Prometheus": 139
Prometheus Bound: 127
Proverbios, Los: of Goya, xxi
Prunela, Dr. Alfonso: 119
publicity: techniques of, 118–119
Puerto, Felipe Carrillo: and Alma
Reed, 127; assassination of, 127;
as theme for frescoes, 143
pulque-shop painting: xix, 120
puppet shows: 126

Quetzalcoatl: 159

races: in Mexico, 104–107
racial conflict. SEE conflict, racial
radio: nature of, 46
Rafael, Josefina: 53
Ramírez, Elodia: 52, 53
Raphael: cartoons of, 153–154
Ravenna: Orozco in, 157
Rebels, The: by Alberto Fuster, 25
"red" battalions: 52
Reed, Alma: and Orozco, xx, 127,
129, 138; and Felipe Carrillo
Puerto, 127; and Eva Sikelianos,
127; and Angelo Sikelianos'
poetry, 127, 128–129, 134
Regis, Hotel: 26
Rembrandt: paintings of, 93
Renoir, Pierre Auguste: influence of,
38
Republica de Argentina [Street]:
8–9
"Resurrection": 134
retables: nature of, 120
Revolution (Mexican): effects of,
29, 54; Orozco's experiences
during, 40–46, 50–51, 51–52,

53–56; course of, 49–56; Dr. Atl in, 50; and art, 96; as subject for Orozco's sketches, 133

Revolution, Constitutional: 52

Revolution, World: and frescoes, 143

revolutionary art: 93

— leaders: conflict among, 49–50

Reyes, General: fate of, 41

Rivera, Diego: compared with Orozco, xix; Orozco on, xx; as pupil of Antonio Fabrés, 11; paintings of, 38; and the mural painters, 86; and Syndicate of Painters and Sculptors, 92; return of, from Europe, 96; and The Joint Groups of the Working-Class Movement, 114

Romans: 107, 148

Rome: influence of, 21; and Greece, 135; Orozco in, 157

Rousseau, Douanier: 88

Ruelas, Julio: 15, 15–16

Russians, White: 138

sailors: aid for, 61; dancing of, 61; tattooing of, 61, 65, 74–75

St. Mark's Cathedral: 157

San Antonio, Texas: 46

San Carlos, Academy of. See Academy of San Carlos

Sánchez Azcona: 30

San Francisco: beauty of, 60; Orozco in, 60–66; Mexicans in, 61; state of art in, 66

San Jacinto: 9

San Sebastián: Orozco in, 157

Santa Anita: open-air school at, 38

Santa Maria del Fiore: 157

Saragossa: Orozco in, 157

School of Higher Studies: 7–8

school of painting, new national: Orozco on, xviii

sciences, arts and: in frescoes, 143–144

sculpture, ice: at Dartmouth, 159

Sculptors, Syndicate of Painters and. See Syndicate of Painters and Sculptors

Secretariat of Public Education: publishing department of, 7–8; and artists, 86

Serrano, Luis G.: 33–34

Sibyl, The: of Sikelianos, 134

Sierra, Justo: as Minister of Public Instruction, 10

Sikelianos, Angelo: as tragic poet, 127; translations of poetry of, 127, 128–129

Sikelianos, Eva: and Alma Reed, 127; salon of, 127–130; and Orozco, 129, 133, 134, 138; and the Roman princess, 135

Simplon: entering Italy by, 157

Siqueiros, Alfaro: xx; in student strike, 30–33, 33–34; and The Vanguard, 53; in New York, 71–72; in Europe, 72, 86, 92–93; and the mural painters, 86; "manifesto" of, 92; and Syndicate of Painters and Sculptors, 92; revolutionary art of, 93; and team painting, 98; and The Machete, 113–114; and Preparatory School murals, 118

Siqueiros, Graciela Amador: 71, 113–114

Sistine Chapel: 16, 157

socialism: and Syndicate of Painters and Sculptors, 92; and art, 93

169